THE HOLY SPIRIT AND ESCHATOLOGY
IN PAUL

THE HOLY SPIRIT
AND ESCHATOLOGY
IN PAUL

by

NEILL Q. HAMILTON

Scottish Journal of Theology Occasional Papers
No. 6

OLIVER AND BOYD LTD.
EDINBURGH: TWEEDDALE COURT
LONDON: 39A WELBECK STREET, W.1

FIRST PUBLISHED . . . 1957

PUBLISHED BY OLIVER AND BOYD LTD.
FOR THE SCOTTISH JOURNAL OF THEOLOGY LTD.
AND PRINTED BY ROBERT CUNNINGHAM AND SONS LTD., ALVA

TO DORIS

CONTENTS

INTRODUCTION

THE FORMAL OCCASION for this study in Pauline theology is the requirement of the University of Basel for the degree of Doctor of Theology. The occasion for this particular subject 'The Holy Spirit and Eschatology in Paul' is more personal. Ever since I first became acquainted with the now long-standing discussion of eschatology inside theological studies, I have wondered what was at stake for the life of the individual Christian. What mood, meaning and moment might eschatology impart to the life of the redeemed if taken seriously? This thesis is an attempt toward an answer to this kind of question.

It was decided to approach this question from the side of the Holy Spirit, because I felt that this would lead more immediately to the heart of the matter. Besides, little has been done with this aspect of eschatology directly. This is interesting in view of the number of years that this eschatological discussion has already consumed. As far back as 1912, Dr Gerhardus Vos, then Professor of New Testament at Princeton Seminary, could write, 'the interpretation of Paul's teaching has strongly felt the influence of the emphasis placed in recent discussion upon the eschatological outlook of the early Church'.[1] His article 'The Eschatological Aspect of the Pauline Conception of the Spirit' was the first study to appear dealing directly with my subject. To my knowledge nothing similar has since appeared.[2] An article by Dr Eduard Schweizer, Professor of New Testament at Zürich, entitled 'Gegenwart des Geistes und eschatologische Hoffnung bei Zarathustra, spaetjuedischen Gruppen, Gnostikern, und den Zeugen des Neuen Testamentes', has appeared in a book of collected studies dedicated to C. H. Dodd.[3] But it deals only very briefly with Paul. In view of the

---

[1] Vos, 'The Eschatological Aspect of the Pauline Conception of the Spirit', 1912, p. 211.

[2] Here attention ought to be directed to the recent study in the Synoptics by C. K. Barrett, *The Holy Spirit and the Gospel Tradition*, 1947.

[3] *The Background of the New Testament and Its Eschatology*, edited by W. D. Davies and D. Daube, Cambridge 1956, pp. 482-508.

relatively untouched nature of the subject, it is hoped that this study will make its own contribution.

Besides attempting to work out the implications of the Holy Spirit and eschatology for Christian life, I shall check my results by making a critical comparison with three representative contemporary views of eschatology in New Testament studies.

I am especially grateful to my teacher, Professor Dr Oscar Cullmann, for his encouragement to take up this subject and for his aid in treating it. His work *Christ and Time* opened up the main issues of the eschatological debate so clearly and treated them so convincingly that my study takes Professor Cullmann's conclusions as a foundation.

I am grateful to Professor Dr Eduard Schweizer for his permission to read his unpublished manuscript of the *Pneuma* article to appear in Kittel's *Woerterbuch*, and of the above-mentioned article on the presence of the Spirit and eschatological hope.

I

THE HOLY SPIRIT AND THE LORD

1. *Christology the key to pneumatology*

AN ATTEMPT to deal with the Spirit in the traditional way as an aspect of the doctrine of the Trinity would be inappropriate to Paul. This is not to deny that the Spirit is for Paul a distinct entity over against the Father and the Son. The problem of the Trinity, which is the occasion of the doctrine of the Trinity, was for Paul no problem.[1] He docs not discuss it. To deal with the Spirit in the tradition of the New Testament is to avoid all speculation about the nature of the being of the Spirit.[2] The viewpoint of the New Testament is consistently that of a concern with redemptive history, and this redemptive history is for the first Christians a 'Christ-process'.[3] 1 Cor. 8.6, with its 'one Lord, Jesus Christ, through whom are all things and we through him', the earliest two-part confession, shows the Christocentric perspective of early Christianity in this regard.[4] It follows that 'wherever the subject of discussion is God's revelatory action . . . there, in the Primitive Christian view, the subject of discussion is Christ'.[5] Thus the common opinion is correct which sees the key to the doctrine of the Spirit in the doctrine of Christ.[6] Consequently our first task is to deal with

---

[1] A trinitarian division of New Testament theology 'runs the risk of introducing into the New Testament a later speculative formulation of questions which is foreign to Primitive Christianity; . . . of obliterating or at least weakening Primitive Christianity's thorough orientation to revelatory and redemptive history'. Cullmann, *Christ and Time*, p. 26.

[2] Buechsel, *Der Geist Gottes im Neuen Testament*, p. 396.

[3] Cullmann, ibid.

[4] Cullmann, *The earliest Christian Confessions*, p. 32.

[5] Cullmann, *Christ and Time*, p. 25.

[6] Barth, *The Doctrine of the Word of God*, VOL. I, PT. I, p. 518, 'to be regarded completely as the Spirit of Christ'; Buechsel, *Der Geist Gottes im NT*, p. 402, 'so bestimmt bei Paulus die Anschauung von der Person Jesu die Anschauung vom Geiste'; Cullmann, *The earliest Christian Confessions*, p. 62, 'the contents of belief relating to God and the Holy Ghost are only the unfolding of faith in Christ'; Dillistone, *The Holy Spirit in the Life of Today*, p. 27, citing Canon Quick, 'there is no teaching about the Spirit of God except in direct connexion with the life and work of the Messiah Jesus'; Michel, *Der Brief an die Roemer*, p. 161, 'die Gebundenheit an Jesus Christus ist das neue und entscheidende Kennzeichen fuer die christliche Geistaussage'. Of a contrary opinion, Fuchs, in sympathy with Bultmann, prefers

those passages which relate the Spirit and Christ. Texts are treated in order of their importance for our thought.

2. 'The Lord is the Spirit'—2 Cor. 3.17

A most striking statement is found in 2 Cor. 3.17 (ὁ δὲ κύριος τὸ πνεῦμά ἐστιν), which in some sense equates the Spirit and the resurrected, exalted Lord.[1] That it is not a simple statement of absolute identity is clear from other assertions of Paul, e.g. 2 Cor. 13.14 and 1 Cor. 6.11 and 12.4-6. The question is, then, in what sense are they identical.

The statement of 2 Cor. 3.17b belongs to the passage which begins with 3.6 where Paul states that his ministry concerns a new covenant (καινῆς διαθήκης).[2] The newness of this covenant compared with the old is that for a written code which kills it substitutes the Spirit which gives life. The verses which follow (7-18), expound the superiority of the new over the old by comparing the splendour or glory which they impart and explain on what basis and by what means the transfer from the old to the new may be made. The splendour (δόξα) of the old was a fading (καταργουμένην) one (3.7), in fact it has faded away (3.10). In contrast the splendour of the dispensation of the Spirit is one which transforms its beholders into ever increasing glory (ἀπὸ δόξης εἰς δόξαν—3.18).[3]

The means or instrument by which the old dispensation transmitted its glory was the law. Moses is the personification of the law (3.15, 'whenever Moses is read'), so that the incident from Exod. 34.33-35 in which Moses' face shone from his conversations with God serves as an apt illustration of the Apostle's point. For just as the Law, personified in Moses, was the instrument on earth of communicating the benefits of the old dispensation, in a similar manner the Spirit is the personification of the new dispensation and the instrument on earth of communicating its benefits. Thus it is appropriate to describe

to start from an analysis of Biblical anthropology, *Christus und der Geist bei Paulus*, p. 37; Cullmann, p. 52, 'the earliest confessions, which under the influence of their employment in baptism subjoin the Holy Ghost, justify their mention of Him likewise in a Christological way'.

[1] Foerster, 'Κύριος', p. 1088: 'Dass Jesus ist κύριος als der Auferweckte, geht durch das ganze Neue Testament.'

[2] Koegel, 'Ὁ κύριος τὸ πνεῦμά ἐστιν', p. 35. 'Schon das ist deutlich, dass v. 17 auf das Fruehere, auf v. 6 zurueckgreift.'

[3] Lietzmann, *An Die Korinther I/II, Handbuch zum Neuen Testament*, J. C. B. Mohr (Paul Siebeck, Tuebingen, 1932³, 2 Cor. 3.18, p. 114, 'die δόξα sich staendig steigert'.

4

the new as a 'dispensation of the Spirit' (3.8). Because of this similarity of function, i.e. communication of benefits, Paul was in the habit of comparing the religion of the Old Testament with that of the New Testament in terms of Law and Spirit (Gal. 3, 5.16-25; Rom. 7, 8). In our passage the Spirit is represented as communicating life (3.6)—life as opposed to the death and condemnation that were the results of the Jewish understanding of the Law. This life is treated in terms of glory.

In addition to the generalisation that the Spirit is the instrument of giving life, 3.17b states that 'where the Spirit of the Lord is, there is freedom'. In connexion with this freedom we shall discover the basis upon which, and the means by which, one may transfer from life under the old Mosaic covenant to life under the new. Freedom refers to freedom from bondage to the Law.[1] The obsession of Israel with the Law as the means of salvation amounts to bondage. This bondage results from an inability to see that the Law is *passé*. This inability is represented by the figure of the veil over the face of Moses (*v.* 13) transferred to be a veil over the understanding of Israel (*v.* 15). If it is asserted that where the Spirit is there is freedom, we must conclude, in view of the context, that the Spirit is the means of enlightening the minds of Israel about the true nature of the Law, the means of removing the veil.

But this enlightening in regard to the true nature of the Law only happens as one realises what has taken its place. Now we see the basis of the freeing from the Law. One turns *from* the Law only as one turns *to* the Lord—'when a man turns to the Lord the veil is removed' (*v.* 16). Or, expressed in terms of *v.* 14, 'only in Christ (ἐν Χριστῷ) is it [the veil] taken away'. Thus one may receive the benefits of the new covenant only on the basis of the earthly ministry and death of Christ (suggested by the title Χριστός) and by virtue of His resurrection and exaltation (suggested by the title Κύριος).

The Lord is not only the basis of the giving of these benefits, He is also their source.[2] The glory comes 'from the Lord' (ἀπὸ κυρίου, *v.* 18). This then explains the usage 'Spirit of the Lord' (τὸ πνεῦμα κυρίου) in *v.* 17. The Spirit is the Spirit of the Lord, because what the Spirit gives can only be given by virtue of the

---

[1] Kennedy, *The Theology of the Epistles*, p. 89: 'When he [Paul] dwells on the source of this . . . energy (of the Spirit), he speaks of Christ.'

[2] Rom. 7.3f, 8.2, Gal. 2.4, 4.21-31, 5.1-13.

work of Christ, and because what the Spirit gives comes from the exalted Lord.

Now we are prepared to understand what is meant by ὁ δὲ κύριος τὸ πνεῦμά ἐστιν—'now the Lord is the Spirit' (*v.* 17). As we have seen, the Spirit performs a function similar to the function of the Law under the old covenant. The Spirit is the agent on earth which communicates the benefits of the new covenant. In connexion with these same benefits of the new covenant, the Lord plays a double role. By virtue of His messianic work He is the basis upon which the benefits may be given. And in His present role as exalted Lord, He is the source of the benefits.[1] What our phrase does, then, is to equate the source of the benefits with the agent of their distribution. The sense of ὁ δὲ κύριος τὸ πνεῦμά ἐστιν then becomes: the Spirit so effectively performs His office of communicating to men the benefits of the risen Christ that for all intents and purposes of faith the Lord Himself is present bestowing grace on His own.[2] The Spirit brings the ascended Lord to earth again. The Spirit bridges the gap between transcendence and immanence. The identity here posited is not ontological, an identity of being, but dynamic, an identity which occurs in redemptive action[3]—just as it is in the case of an actor who becomes so absorbed in his role and plays it so skilfully that we forget the actor himself and he becomes for us the person he is portraying. It is in just this sense that the Lord is the Spirit. The Spirit portrays the Lord so well that we lose sight of the Spirit and are conscious of the Lord only.[4] This suggests the following pattern of redemptive

[1] It is obvious that the whole argument turns upon the process of communicating the benefits of redemption to believers. Thus Koegel is correct when he points ('Ὁ κύριος τὸ πνεῦμά ἐστιν', p. 43) to the soteriological as the crux of the matter: 'Die Identitaet [between the Lord and the Spirit] hat speziell in soteriologischer Beziehung statt.'

[2] E. Schweizer, 'Πνεῦμα', III, 1, *b*: 'Insofern Christus in seiner Bedeutung fuer die Gemeinde, in seinem kraftvollen Handeln an ihr gesehen wird, kann er mit dem πνεῦμα identifiziert werden.' Windisch, *Der Zweite Korintherbrief*, p. 124, followed by Buechsel, *Der Geist Gottes im NT*, p. 409, accurately describes it as a 'dynamic identification', i.e. an identification which occurs in redemptive action.

[3] Koegel, 'Ὁ κύριος τὸ πνεῦμά ἐστιν', p 44: 'die Aussage 2 Kor. 3, 17 ... hat ... nicht eine metaphysische, sondern eine soteriologische Bedeutung.'

[4] This self-veiling of the Spirit may lead to confusion about the personality of the Spirit—especially in connexion with the concept of power. As is becoming evident, the Spirit is pre-eminently the One who throws light upon Christ. Therefore in all His action He seeks to fill the consciousness of men with the picture of Christ—and to do this He must avoid making *Himself* the object of consciousness. This kind of phenomenon, i.e. the Spirit producing effects without making His own nature evident, we call power. We do not 'see' power in operation. We only see effects and deduce from these effects that power is present. Thus power is an

action: from the Lord—through the Spirit—to the believer. That this exegesis faithfully represents Paul's thought becomes clear from a glance at each of the three communicated benefits which Paul describes in this same passage.

Life is the first gift that he mentions (*v.* 6, τὸ δὲ πνεῦμα ζῳοποιεῖ).[1] The Spirit performs the function noted above. He distributes or communicates the benefits of the new covenant— in this case 'life'—to men. What is the source or basis of this gift of life? According to Col. 3.3-4 and Rom. 8.2, it is Christ.[2] The believer's life is 'hid with Christ in God' (Col. 3.3), and Christ is the believer's life (*v.* 4). Our exegesis is supported. The pattern of redemptive action in the case of 'life' is from Christ, through the Spirit, to the believer. The Spirit is the channel of the 'life' which is stored in Christ.

2 Cor. 3.17*b* makes the Spirit the mediator of 'freedom'. Freedom in our passage especially refers to freedom from the Law (*v.* 6), which brings death (*v.* 7). In Rom. 8.2 Paul refers to freedom in the same terms and attributes this freedom to the action of the Spirit. In Gal. 5, he also represents freedom as freedom from the Law in the concrete instance of circumcision.[3] In the same chapter he bases the gift of freedom on Christ: 'for freedom Christ has set us free' (Gal. 5.1). And in Rom. 8.2, just as we saw life based on Christ, so also the law of the Spirit, which sets free, is based on Christ. Christ is the source. The Spirit is the agent of distribution. But that which the Spirit communicates remains a property of Christ. Thus through redemptive action the Spirit and the Lord are identified.

An understanding of the source and agent of glory, leads us to the same conclusion. The glory is the glory of the Lord (2 Cor. 3.18) and is to be seen in the face of Jesus Christ (4.6). In Eph. 3.16 the Apostle prays that the Spirit may be for the believer a channel of the riches of God's glory, and the inner strength of this glory is to come 'through the Spirit', διὰ τοῦ πνεύματος.

especially appropriate description for the Spirit. His work of revealing Chirst is by nature self-effacing, mysterious, lest in the performance of His office He should detract men from Christ.

[1] 1 Cor. 15.45 connects the same verb with the Spirit—πνεῦμα ζῳοποιοῦν.

[2] 2 Tim. 1.10, Christ has brought life to light; 1 Tim. 1.1, life is *in* Christ Jesus. Paul can say that the life which he has now is not his own, but that Christ lives in him (Gal. 1.19f; Rom. 8.10); that His life is in us (2 Cor. 4.10f); or that we live in Christ (Rom. 6.11) and shall live—in Him—(2 Cor. 13.4); that our life is in Christ (Rom. 8.2). Bultmann, 'Ζάω', in Kittel, BAND II, p. 869.

[3] Schlier, ''Ελεύθερος', in Kittel, BAND II, p. 493.

7

In connexion with the passage 2 Cor. 3.6-17 it only remains to be noted that in *v.* 18 ἀπὸ κυρίου πνεύματος should be interpreted 'by the Spirit of the Lord'.[1] As such it is an echo and reinforcement of the point already made in *v.* 17. For purposes of communicating redemption the Lord and the Spirit are one.

It is appropriate and understandable that this identification of the Lord and the Spirit should have been made in a letter to the Corinthians, who were so engrossed with the wealth and variety of their spiritual experience that they were in danger of losing sight of the fact that the basis of all Christian spirituality is Christ.

3. 'No one can say Jesus is Lord except by the Holy Spirit'—1 Cor. 12.3

This same motif is at work in 1 Cor. 12.3. Paul proposes to deal with spiritual gifts (*v.* 1). But at the outset he wants it clearly held in mind that what distinguishes any pre-Christian, heathen spirituality the Corinthians might have had from their experiences of the Spirit as Christians is the Christocentricity of the action of the Spirit. The first and primary action of the Spirit which is the prerequisite of all His other action is that the Spirit brings one to a recognition of the fact that 'Jesus is Lord' (*ΚΥΡΙΟΣ ΙΗΣΟΥΣ*). Paul's use of the word εἰπεῖν ('to say') rather than ὁμολογεῖν shows that he is not necessarily restricting his view to the special case of being able to confess Jesus Lord in the face of martyrdom.[2] He is concerned with the fact that anyone, in any circumstances, should come to be a Christian at all, and this he attributes to the action of the Spirit

---

[1] Windisch, *Der zweite Korintherbrief*, p. 129, and Lietzmann, *An die Galater*, p. 114, read 'from the Lord of the Spirit'. Buechsel, *Der Geist Gottes im NT*, p. 407, reads 'Lord who is the Spirit'. In the case of the first possibility, it seems to me improbable that Paul would introduce a new idea of such weight as 'Lord of the Spirit' implies without more occasion than a final twist to the last phrase of the whole section. The second possibility is discouraged by the lack of an article for πνεύματος, which would be expected in the case of apposition (see Blass and Debrunner, *Grammatik des neutestamentlichen Griechisch*, para. 268, p. 167), although it must be admitted that the article can fall out after prepositions (Blass and Debrunner, para. 255, p. 159). In such cases as this the rules of grammar do not *compel* a particular solution, but the reading chosen fits those rules best.

[2] That this confession did at times have special reference to witness under persecution is clear from the contrasting form *ΑΝΑΘΕΜΑ ΙΗΣΟΥΣ* mentioned in the same verse. That its use was not *confined* to persecution situations is shown by its broad significance for primitive Christianity. The persecutions did however force the Church to single out the crux of its faith. See Cullmann, *The earliest Christian Confessions*, p. 28f, for the historic origins of this formula, and p. 55f, for its significance for all of primitive Christianity. This formula appeared also in the liturgy of worship and in exorcism.

8

($ἐν$ $πνεύματι$ $ἁγίῳ$). That this is the case is shown by the place this particular expression, 'Jesus is Lord', had in primitive Christianity. The conclusion to which Professor Cullman comes finally in *The earliest Christian Confessions* is crucial for a full appreciation of our passage[1]:

It is, then, the *present* Lordship of Christ, inaugurated by His resurrection and exaltation to the right hand of God, that is the centre of the faith of primitive Christianity. The affirmation of the present reign of Christ, and of the power in heaven and on earth conferred upon Him, is the historical and dogmatic core of the Christian confession, which we were to seek. Its simplest expression is the formula *Kyrios Christos*.

So nothing less is asserted in our passage than that the Spirit is responsible for the faith of primitive Christianity.[2] Whatever it was that possessed the Corinthians before their conversion the main fact about it was that it led them to idols (*v.* 2). What possesses them now is the Spirit, and the main thing about that experience is that it leads them to Christ (*v.* 3).[3] The Spirit's relationship with faith and spiritual gifts to which this verse points will be discussed more thoroughly in the sections relating to the spiritual life of the individual and the Church. For the moment it suffices to note the Christocentric foundation for all action of the Spirit which Paul here lays. The Spirit not only transmits the benefits of Christ and so makes Christ present to faith, but also promotes that recognition of the Lordship of Jesus which is the birth of faith. 'The importance which the Spirit has for Paul arises out of the fact that through Him the sending of Christ actually becomes a revelation of divine grace.'[4]

---

[1] Cullmann, *The earliest Christian Confessions*, p. 58.

[2] Gunkel, *Die Wirkungen des heiligen Geistes*, p. 71, objects that that particular function through which a man becomes a Christian is nowhere expressly designated as work of the Spirit. Rather (citing Gal. 3.14) he ascribes to Paul the view that faith is the presupposition of the receipt of the Spirit. Schlier, *Der Brief an die Galater*, p. 81, comments on *v.* 2 that Paul in this section is not handling the question in which way and by what means the Spirit is communicated to the Church. In *v.* 2 both the Spirit and faith are conditional on preaching ($ἀκοή$, cp. Rom. 10.14). The faith mentioned in *v.* 14 is not the condition of receiving the Spirit but 'the manner in which the given Spirit is experienced' (Schlier, *Der Brief an die Galater*, p. 97). If this passage does not attribute faith to the Spirit, it is difficult to imagine what is attributed to the Spirit. The lack of the verb $ὁμολογῶ$ eliminates the possibility that only the power for public confession is being considered here (1 Cor. 12.3). For a parallel situation, see Matt. 16.16, 17. Buechsel, *Der Geist Gottes im NT*, p. 309, goes so far as to conclude that 'faith is for Paul something pneumatic'. Compare Eph. 1.13.

[3] E. Schweizer concludes, unequivocally, (*Geist und Gemeinde im NT und Heute*, p. 20) that the Spirit 'is the power which gives us faith in Jesus Christ'.

[4] A. Schlatter, *Die Theologie des NT*, BAND II, p. 322.

4. 'Anyone who does not have the Spirit of Christ does not belong to him'—Rom. 8.9*b*

The conclusion drawn from the exegesis of 2 Cor. 3.7, namely, that it is the Spirit which brings the resurrected Lord to the believer, is again expressed in Rom. 8.9-10, where Spirit is spoken of as dwelling—οἰκεῖ (*vv.* 9, 11) and ἐνοικοῦντος (*v.* 11) —in the believer, and the believer has (ἔχει) the Spirit (*v.* 9). Then with no warning the very same phenomenon is described as Christ being in the believer—Χριστός ἐν ὑμῖν (*v.* 10).[1] This reveals that in Paul's mind they mean the same thing. The resulting identification of the Spirit and Christ is parallel to 2 Cor. 3.17: 'the Lord is the Spirit' (ὁ δὲ κύριος τὸ πνεῦμά ἐστιν). The terms 'Christ' and 'the Spirit of Christ' are used interchangeably.[2] But once again it is not necessarily an ontological identification of being: here, too, it is in fact a dynamic identification.[3] Those who mean to live in the Spirit, and not in the flesh, have Christ in them, and on the basis of his righteousness (*v.* 10) they are guaranteed life—though sin may still bring the body to death. Christ is introduced into the argument at *v.* 10, in order to show that it was His messianic work that is the basis for the Spirit's activities. The Spirit gives His gift of life to what is mortal on the basis of Christ's righteousness and after the pattern of Christ's resurrection. The Spirit applies the benefits of Christ, but since those benefits are inseparable from the living Lord, the Lord Himself is present. If Paul were not careful occasionally to assert this dynamic identification, the error might arise of supposing that one could have the benefits of Christ's redemption without a personal relationship with Him and with the accompanying claims and demands of His Lordship. The gifts of the Spirit of Christ are only at the disposal of those who have placed themselves at Christ's disposal.

Christ is also introduced into the argument at *v.* 9, again in order to tie the Spirit's activities to Christ.

Rom. 8.9*b*, 'Anyone who does not have the Spirit of Christ does not belong to him', adds a new element to our understanding of the relation of the Spirit and Christ, which is similar to

---

[1] Michel, *Der Brief an die Römer*, p. 163, 'the sentence structure of *v.* 10 shows a strong parallelism'.

[2] Headlam and Sanday, *The Epistle to the Romans*, p. 197.

[3] 'Here . . . is simply meant, that, where the Spirit is at work, Christ also works and vice versa.' Gaugler, *Der Roemerbrief, Prophezei*, i, p. 275.

the point of 1 Cor. 12.3. 1 Cor. 12.3 credited the Spirit with
our connexion with Christ in the matter of faith. 2 Cor. 3.17
credited the Spirit with making Christ present to the believer,
bestowing life, freedom, and glory. Rom. 8.9b draws these both
together. It states that the Spirit is the connecting link between
Christ and the believer in every respect. It implies that Christ
has no access to men outside of His Spirit. Anybody who does
not have the Spirit simply 'is not his' (οὐκ ἔστιν αὐτοῦ). This
makes it apparent why an understanding of the Spirit's work
is necessary for an understanding of the life of the individual
Christian and of the Church. The Spirit is the Spirit of Christ
because He relates men to Christ.

5. 'The Spirit of his Son'—Gal. 4.6

Gal. 4.6 is a repetition of the idea of the Spirit as the link
between Christ and the believer viewed from the angle of sonship. 'The basic function of the Spirit of God is obviously to
secure the relationship of faith to its object, Jesus Christ. Out
of this relation of faith to Christ result the specific possibilities
of Christian action with its accompanying Christian knowledge.'[1] According to 4.6, the Spirit makes the objective possibility of sonship to God a subjective reality in the believer—
witness the expression of one who knows and feels himself to be
really a child of God[2] in the cry, 'Abba, Father'.[3] In this instance the Spirit performs His function of establishing a relationship between the believer and Christ in order that we should
share the same attitude to the Father as does Christ.[4] The cry
is the cry of Jesus in Gethsemane.[5]

[1] Fuchs, *Christus und der Geist bei Paulus*, p. 40.
[2] Exactly the same expression is attributed to the Spirit in Rom. 8.16, but in
v. 15 the Spirit is described according to the effect of His action—sonship—rather
than according to the basis of that sonship—Christ (πνεῦμα υἱοθεσίας).
[3] Schlier, *Der Brief an die Galater*, p. 139, argues that we are sons of God prior to
the giving of the Spirit. Lietzmann (*An die Galater*, p. 27) prefers to read '*that* (ὅτι)
you however [now actually] are sons', and argues convincingly by comparison with
Rom. 8.15, 16 that the cry is an evidence of sonship—not that sonship precedes the
Spirit. Schlier's view provides no vehicle for the relationship of sonship. A purely
forensic sonship would be incongruous.
[4] It is interesting to note in connexion with 1 Cor. 12.3, that in relating the
Spirit to Christ's 'divine sonship', we relate the Spirit to the second of the two
essential elements in the majority of the confessions of the first century. Cullmann,
The earliest Christian Confessions, p. 57.
[5] Barth, *The Doctrine of the Word of God*, VOL. I, PT. I, p. 524. 'It is marvellously,
but of a surety not accidentally, the same cry which the Gospel narrative (Mark
14.36) puts in the mouth of Jesus in Gethsemane.'

6. 'The Spirit of Jesus Christ'—Phil. 1.19

Paul here contemplates the possibility of a martyr's death. Come what may he will honour Christ in life or death (*v.* 20). His only assurance against martyrdom is the possibility that he is still needed for service (1.25, 2.24). He expects the Spirit to be his equipment (ἐπιχορηγίας) (Phil. 1.19) against losing his relationship with Christ in the face of death and the urge to deny Him. In 2 Cor. 3.18 (perhaps autobiographically) and 1 Cor. 12.3 Paul spoke of the function of the Spirit in initiating one's relation with Christ. Now in contemplating the final test of that relationship he again looks to the Spirit. It is a touching commentary on the part Paul's understanding of the Spirit played in his own experience. The Spirit that attended his conversion (2 Cor. 3.18, 1 Cor. 12.3), showed him the way to rise above the flesh (Rom. 8.9), gave him evidence of his adoption as a son (Gal. 4.5), and will now support him at the end.

7. The Spirit and the Resurrection—Exaltation

The passages treated so far show that the Spirit is the Spirit of Christ because the Spirit's office is confined to revealing and communicating Christ to the believer. The Spirit is the Spirit of Christ dynamically, i.e. in the process of redemptive action they become identical. The Spirit mediates the presence of Christ. But the question might still be raised: is their relation merely *functional*, or is there a deeper sense in which it is *appropriate* that they should be so linked together for purposes of redeeming mankind? Our answer will be found in the passages which relate the Spirit to the resurrection and exaltation of Christ. In these it will be seen that the Spirit is *appropriately* the Spirit of Christ in redemptive action because He was the Spirit of Christ prior to any redemptive action.[1]

Rom. 1.4 makes clear the fact that the Spirit is the equipment of Christ's exaltation as Lord. *Vv.* 1-4 progressively develop what Paul's gospel has to say about Christ. In *v.* 1, Jesus is the Messiah. In *v.* 3, the Messiah is God's Son. In *v.* 4*a* this Messiah, Jesus, whose sonship was veiled in the days of His flesh is suddenly revealed as 'Son of God in power', i.e. He attains

---

[1] Here 'redemptive' is used in the sense of actually imparting to man the benefits of God's saving acts in Christ.

openly to the full dignity and status of deity.[1] This final and climactic stage in the progressive revelation of Jesus is expressed by the term 'Lord' (*v.* 4*b*), which sums up all the glory and majesty which early Christianity ascribed to the resurrected and exalted Lord, and is synonymous with 'Son of God in power' (*v.* 4*a*). Here again we meet the earliest Christian confession, 'Jesus is Lord.'

The words 'according to the Spirit of holiness' (κατὰ πνεῦμα ἁγιωσύνης) explain this new state. They stand in contrast to the words 'according to the flesh' (κατὰ σάρκα), which describe Christ's mode of being before the resurrection. 'Paul then distinguishes two different modes of Christ's existence which by no means lie on the same plane.'[2] The flesh was the vehicle of Christ's existence before the resurrection. The Holy Spirit is now the vehicle, the mode, the manner of His status as Lord. This will be seen to be of decisive importance for the relationship of eschatology and the Holy Spirit.

This new relationship of the Spirit to the Lord occurred 'since' or 'on the basis of' the resurrection[3] (ἐξ ἀναστάσεως νεκρῶν). The idea of 'since' is obviously present here, but to decide whether and in what sense the resurrection could be not only the beginning but also the ground of this new existence of Christ, we turn to the passages which link the Spirit with the resurrection. They do this indirectly, by means of the concepts of 'glory' and 'power' associated with the Spirit.[4]

In 1 Cor. 6.14, Paul tells us that 'God raised the Lord and will also raise us up by his power' (διὰ τῆς δυνάμεως αὐτοῦ).

---

[1] Headlam and Sanday, *The Epistle to the Romans*, p. 9, connect ἐν δυνάμει not with υἱοῦ θεοῦ but with ὁρισθέντος, thus missing the whole point of Paul's progressive development of Christ's status. To connect 'in power' with 'designate' would be redundant. 'Ὁρισθέντος is forceful enough in itself to complete its meaning without adverbs. It means 'effectual appointment'. Vos, 'The Eschatological Aspect of the Pauline Conception of the Spirit', p. 229, 'jemanden zu etwas bestellen'. Lietzmann, *An die Galater*, p. 25, 'ἐν δυνάμει belongs rather with υἱοῦ θεοῦ'. Michel, *Der Brief an die Römer*, p. 31, 'δύναμις is used exactly like δόξα as God's form of appearance'.

[2] The common consensus of opinion today in the exegesis of this verse holds to two different forms of existence which, for example, correspond to Phil. 2.5-11, Michel, op. cit., p. 32. Nygren, *Commentary on Romans*, p. 51: 'So the resurrection is the turning point in the existence of the Son of God. Before that He was the Son of God in weakness and lowliness. Through the resurrection he became the Son of God in power.'

[3] Michel, op. cit., p. 32, prefers 'on the basis of the resurrection'. Lietzmann, op. cit., p. 26, reads 'since the resurrection'. Both are possible.

[4] Vos, 'The Eschatological Aspect of the Pauline Conception of the Spirit', p. 234. For a development of thought similar to this whole section, see Vos, pp. 228-35.

Taken in conjunction with the teaching (Rom. 8.11) that the medium of the believer's life after his resurrection will be the Spirit, this means that the same Spirit which will sustain the life of the believer after his resurrection will also have been responsible for the resurrection itself. If this will be true of the believer, we may infer that the same is already true in the case of Christ. Rom. 6.4 implies directly that the Spirit not only characterises and sustains Christ's exaltation as Lord, but was also the agent of His resurrection. 'Christ was raised from the dead by the glory of the Father' (διὰ τῆς δόξης τοῦ πατρός). 'By the glory of the Father' is probably a formal, and perhaps a liturgical phrase. Glory suggests the state to which Christ attained at His exaltation, and behind that state lies the Spirit. Then we may conclude that that same Spirit is the agent at work behind the glory which raised up Christ. 2 Cor. 13.4 teaches that the Spirit must continually sustain the life He gave to Christ at the resurrection. In some sense Christ needs the Spirit as a manner of life after the resurrection in the same way as He needed flesh for His manner of life in earth. Christ 'lives by the power of God' (ζῇ ἐκ δυνάμεως θεοῦ). These three passages give an account of the work of the Spirit in terms of which we are justified in ascribing the resurrection as well as the exaltation life to the Spirit. The resurrection and exaltation are but two sides of the one continuous act of the Spirit whereby Jesus was raised from death to the exaltation life of His Lordship. In Rom. 1.4, ἐξ ἀναστάσεως νεκρῶν means that the life of the exalted Lord both dates from and is based on the resurrection since the Spirit is responsible for both the life and the resurrection. The exegesis of one additional passage completes the treatment of the Spirit and the Lord.

In 1 Cor. 15.45, Paul states that the last Adam, meaning Christ, became a life-giving Spirit (ἐγένετο εἰς πνεῦμα ζωοποιοῦν). The 'becoming' (ἐγένετο) of the first half of the verse applies obviously to this second half. This assertion about Christ is a parallel to the creation of man in Gen. 2.7, which is quoted in the first half of the verse. In the light of what we have seen of Paul's thought in this regard, a 'becoming', predicted of Christ, which results in His identification with the Spirit, can only refer to what occurred at His resurrection. In 2 Cor. 3.17 we saw that the Spirit was identical with the Lord (i.e., the resurrected exalted Christ). Rom. 1.4 made it clear that this life of resurrection and exaltation came after and as a result of the resurrection. What we have behind this short verse is a striking and illuminating parallel between what occurred at creation and what occurred at Christ's resurrection.[1] In the same way that God breathed the breath of life into the man of dust so that that breath and man's life became synonymous, so also at Christ's resurrection the Father breathed the Holy Spirit into His dead Son so that He lived and so that that Spirit and the life of the resurrected Christ became synonymous.

Here we see the Spirit and Christ identified in a remarkably intimate way which goes beyond all dynamic explanations. The Spirit *is* the resurrection and exaltation of the Lord. In His resurrection and exaltation the Lord is not merely equipped with the Spirit, like a prophet, to fulfil a particular office and to perform certain appointed functions. The Lord is 'equipped' with the Spirit in the same way as a man is 'equipped' with life. The grace or the gospel in this fact is that Christ's life of resurrection and exaltation is a communicable one. It is not confined to Christ. It is a life that can make others alive. It is a *life-giving* Spirit (πνεῦμα ζωοποιοῦν).

This does not nullify the exegesis of those passages in which we saw expressed a functional, dynamic relation between the Spirit and Christ. Rather it provides the deeper insight which explains why this relationship is appropriate. The Spirit is the redeemer Spirit for the believer, because it was in a sense the redeemer Spirit for the Lord Himself.

Summary

Our exegesis of the passages which relate the Spirit and Christ have confirmed our presupposition that Paul's doctrine of the Spirit is Christocentric.

The Spirit is the Spirit of Christ because His office is to communicate the benefits of Christ's work. But since Christ's gifts are inseparable from His person, the Spirit mediates the presence of the Lord. Thus from the standpoint of faith the Spirit and the Lord are identical. The pattern of redemptive action is: from the Lord, through the Spirit, to the believer.

The Spirit and the Lord are related in still a deeper sense.

[1] In sharp disagreement with Weiss, *Der Erste Korintherbrief,* p. 374, who makes the second part of the verse a part of Paul's quotation, without however explaining its origin. Deissner, *Auferstehungshoffnung und Pneumagedanke bei Paulus,* pp. 40ff, also relates *v.* 45*b* to the resurrection.

The Spirit raised Christ and is His life of exaltation. The same Spirit which gave life at the resurrection continues to sustain it afterward. Therefore we conclude that the Spirit is the channel of the Lord's life in redemptive action because the Spirit is that life.

The genitive which connects the Spirit and the Lord is both possessive and qualifying.[1] It is possessive in the sense that the Spirit has been given to the Lord as the equipment, the power to fulfil the office of Lord. It is qualifying in the sense that the Spirit is the life of the Lord.

When in the following section we set the Spirit and the resurrection in the context of Paul's eschatology we shall see that what we have discovered so far will have tremendous consequences for the understanding of the nature of the life of the individual believer and the Church.

[1] The Spirit—of Christ, of Jesus Christ, of His Son.

II

THE HOLY SPIRIT AND TIME

THIS CHAPTER is intended to relate the Spirit to the continuous time-line of the New Testament. The attempt will be made to show that the Spirit is related primarily to the future, to eternity, to the time of the consummation of the redemptive process.

1. *Christ's Resurrection—Exaltation and the General Resurrection*

That the Spirit belongs primarily to the future was implicit in the last section of the preceding chapter. By linking the Spirit with the resurrected, exalted Lord, Paul automatically links the Spirit with the future. If the Spirit inaugurated and sustains the life of the resurrected Lord, then the Spirit will also inaugurate and sustain the life of the redeemed in their resurrection. This is true because Paul sees in the exalted Lord the realisation already of the future of the redeemed. The Lord's resurrection is continuous with the general resurrection.

This idea is apparent in Rom. 1.4 in the phrase ἐξ ἀναστάσεως νεκρῶν. This is an expression which describes the general resurrection.[1] It implies that this future general resurrection has already begun with Christ's resurrection.[2] This fact comes to explicit expression in 1 Cor. 15.20, 23, and Col. 1.18, where the relation of the resurrected Christ to the whole company of the dead is described with the words: ἀπαρχή, ἀρχή, and πρωτότοκος. Ἀπαρχή means 'first-fruits' and refers to the earliest crop of the year.[3] It implies an identity in kind with more fruit to come from the same source in the same season. It is at the same time

---

[1] Michel's contention, *Der Brief an die Römer*, p. 31, n. 1, is that in *vv.* 3-4, the contrast between κατὰ σάρκα and κατὰ πνεῦμα ἁγιωσύνης suggests the two ages into which Jewish eschatology divided time. In support he points out that the concepts power, Spirit of holiness, and resurrection of the dead are all distinguishing marks of the new age. So also Vos, 'The Eschatological Aspect of the Pauline Conception of the Spirit', p. 230.

[2] For Paul the resurrection of Christ is the beginning of the resurrection of the dead. Through Christ the resurrection age has burst upon us. Nygren, *Commentary on Romans*, p. 50.

[3] Delling, ''Ἀπαρχή', in Kittel, BAND I, p. 484. Bauer, Walter, *Griechisch-Deutsches Woerterbuch*, p. 147. Lietzmann, *Korinther I/II*, p. 79.

a sign that this other fruit will soon appear. 'Αρχή means simply 'beginning', and implies a temporal process to follow which according to πρωτεύων in the same verse is somehow dependent on this beginning.[1] Πρωτότοκος means 'first-born', and suggests others to come of the same family.[2] These three concepts all have one point in common. They tie the resurrection and resurrection life of Christ into a common process with the future resurrection of believers. The obvious conclusion is that the Spirit which lay behind the resurrection and exaltation of the Lord will also constitute the future life of believers. It is important in this regard to note that Christ's present resurrection and exaltation are regarded from the standpoint of the general resurrection of the future. The emphasis is placed on the future and the present is to be understood in that light. This exhibits the point we are attempting to prove. The activity of the Spirit we know in Christ belongs properly to the future and is understandable only as a property of the future age. Thus we see that Michel's relating of Rom. 1.4 to the two ages has support when viewed in a wider context of Paul's thought.

2. *'He who raised up Christ Jesus from the dead will give life to your mortal bodies also through his Spirit which dwells in you'*—Rom. 8.11

This verse is the complement of Rom. 1.14. Whereas in 1.14 Jesus' resurrection was attributed directly to the agency of the Spirit, and the general resurrection only indirectly, in 8.11 the general resurrection is attributed directly to the agency of the Spirit, while Christ's resurrection is attributed indirectly to the Spirit. The crucial phrase is διὰ τοῦ ἐνοικοῦντος αὐτοῦ πνεύματος in which διὰ with the genitive must be translated 'through', and leaves no doubt that here the agency of the Spirit in the future resurrection of the redeemed is intended.[3] There is, however,

---

[1] 'The word "beginning" transposes into time what the word "head" means in relation to the organism', Lohmeyer, *Die Briefe an die Philipper, an die Kolosser und an Philemon*, p. 62. Contrary to Delling, s.v. ἀρχή in Kittel BAND I, p. 482, who renders ἀρχή as something similar in meaning to the Stoic teaching of an all-pervasive world principle.

[2] Lohmeyer, op. cit., p. 62. Dibelius, *An die Kolosser, Epheser, an Philemon*, p. 17, thinks that this word refers to the new humanity which began with Christ's resurrection.

[3] Good evidence is present for the accusative case which would change the reading to 'on account of'—thus Gaugler, *Der Römerbrief, Prophezei*, I, pp. 280-1. Michel, Schlatter, Sanday and Headlam, Cullmann (*Christ and Time*, p. 237), and Nygren prefer the accusative. Sanday and Headlam, in *The Epistle to the Romans*,

the possibility of another reading. If we prefer the accusative —διὰ τὸ ἐνοικοῦν αὐτοῦ πνεῦμα—there is the added thought that the Spirit not only initiates the resurrection but also sustains in their resurrection the life of the redeemed. In this passage the Apostle repeats the idea of Ezek. 37.14, which was recognised in late Judaism as being of continuing eschatological importance.[1] Here in Rom. 8.11 we have begun to encounter those passages which unequivocally assert the primarily future character of the Spirit.

3. The Spirit as ἀπαρχή and ἀρραβών

Rom. 8.23 carries forward the thought of 8.11. The Spirit is related to another aspect of the future, namely the renewal of material creation (v. 21). The genitive ἀπαρχὴν τοῦ πνεύματος identifies the 'Spirit' with 'first-fruits'.[2] This description of the Spirit as ἀπαρχή integrates the Spirit into the future age through the renewal of the material creation in the specific instance of the bodies of the redeemed. The gift of the Spirit in the present is to be understood as only the beginning of the harvest proper which will occur in the new creation of the future age. Because the centre of gravity lies in the future, the sons of God groan in the present. The harvest of redemption has only just begun. Therefore, as Gunkel points out, 'the presupposition here is that the Spirit is the present and future possession of the Christian; a partial bestowal in the present which proves a complete bestowal in the future'.[3]

Using the figure of harvest, but with a different twist, Gal. 6.8 also relates the Spirit directly to the future by picturing the Spirit as the source and basis of eternal life. 'He who sows to the Spirit will of the Spirit reap eternal life.' In this figure of harvest the Spirit represents the soil rather than the crops. The result is the same as before—'eternally enduring life will be an

pp. 198, 199, summarise the evidences for both readings and point out that while the accusative reading is Western, it is important that the Alexandrian genitive reading is attested as far west as Hippolytus. Sokolowski, *Die Begriffe Geist und Leben bei Paulus*, pp. 55, 56, draws attention to the fact that both readings lead to the same conclusion, namely that the Spirit is of decisive importance for the coming into existence of the future life. So also Vos, 'The eschatological Aspect of the Pauline Conception of the Spirit', p. 226.

[1] See Strack-Billerbeck, *Kommentar zum Neuen Testament aus Talmud und Midrasch*, BAND III, p. 241.

[2] Schlatter, *Gottes Gerechtigkeit*, p. 275, and Michel, *Der Brief an die Römer*, p. 176. Both show how another construction is mistaken. Compare Gunkel, *Die Wirkungen des heiligen Geistes*, p. 63 n. 1.

[3] Gunkel, op. cit., p. 63.

effect of the Spirit'.[1] Thus we conclude that since the Spirit is the ground of the eschatological life of the future, the Spirit belongs primarily to the future.[2]

2 Cor. 5.5 describes the Spirit as a guarantee (ἀρραβών) of the eternal, heavenly dwelling (vv. 1-2) of the future state. 1.22 uses the same term to show that the Spirit is our assurance that God's promises (v. 20) will be fulfilled. In Eph. 1.14 the term is again used in an eschatological context to show that the Spirit is 'the guarantee of our inheritance until we acquire possession of it'. This threefold connexion of the Spirit, by means of the concept ἀρραβών, (1) to the resurrection body of the redeemed, (2) to the fulfilment of God's promises, and (3) to the inheritance of redemption, brings us to the heart of Paul's conception of the Spirit. It belongs primarily to the future. 'Αρραβών is a term which Paul has coined specifically to express the primarily eschatological nature of the Spirit.[3] Were all the other considerations set forth in this chapter inapplicable, this concept would bear the weight of proof almost alone. Because of its crucial importance for this whole thesis the observations of others on this ἀρραβών concept deserve our attention. Professor Cullmann states[4]:

We have seen the Spirit is an element of the future aeon, the matter out of which the new creation of God's kingdom will consist internally as well as externally. This constituent part of the future Kingdom of God is already there in the Church, only, however, as a 'down payment' (ἀρραβών, 2 Cor.1.22).

And again[5]:

Paul draws emphatic attention to the fact that the Spirit presents the piece of the future that has now already become present when he designates it as 'first-fruits' (ἀπαρχή, Rom. 8.23) and as 'down payment' (ἀρραβών, 2 Cor. 1.22).

C. K. Barrett expresses the same idea[6]:

For Paul also, the gift of the Spirit meant both the realisation of eschatology and a reaffirmation of it; so much is implied by his use of the

[1] Sokolowski, Die Begriffe Geist und Leben bei Paulus, p. 53. See also Vos, 'The eschatological Aspect of the Pauline Conception of the Spirit', pp. 220-7.
[2] 'ζωὴ αἰώνιος is eschatological', Schlier, Der Brief an die Galater, p. 204.
[3] Compare non-theological use in Gen. 39.17, 11. 'Just as in the early Church Paul's evaluation of the gifts of the Spirit as a guarantee for the truth of the gospel has an eschatological point', Gunkel, Die Wirkungen des heiligen Geistes, p. 63. n. 1.
[4] Cullmann, Koenigsherrschaft Christi und Kirche im Neuen Testament, p. 23.
[5] Cullmann, op. cit., p. 20.
[6] Barrett, The Holy Spirit and the Gospel Tradition, p. 153.

term ἀρραβών; the present possession of the Spirit means that part of the future bliss is already attained, and equally that part still remains future, still unpossessed.

Eduard Schweizer writes[1]:

If the decisive event is on the one hand the resurrection of Jesus and on the other hand the resurrection of the believers, then the Spirit must be understood, as in the early Church, as a sign for what is still to come. Since the event of Jesus' resurrection, the resurrection at the end of the times is no longer an indefinite hope; the reality of the present Spirit guarantees the reality of what is to come. Thus can Paul designate the πνεῦμα as ἀπαρχή for the still to be expected redemption of the body (Rom. 8.23) or as ἀρραβών for the new 'house' which waits for us (2 Cor. 5.5, 1.22).

Behm comments on the common thrust of the ἀρραβών passages: 'The Spirit, which God has given them, is security to the Christians for the future, complete possession of salvation.' And, finally, Gunkel says: 'The Spirit is the preliminary payment, which ought to be a guarantee for the future, complete payment, which is still outstanding (2 Cor. 1.22, 5.5; cf. Eph. 1.14).'[2]

4. *The Spirit and the Kingdom of God*

Rom. 14.17 connects the kingdom of God with the Spirit. Whether or not this relates the Spirit to the future depends on one's understanding of Paul's use of the concept of kingdom of God. Paul's use of it is much more straightforward than the use in the *Gospels*. With him it is clear that the kingdom of God is still outstanding. It is the sphere of the future blessings of redemption. This is immediately evident from the fact that the kingdom of God is described as something to be inherited or an inheritance (κληρονομία, κληρονομεῖν) in five of the ten passages where it appears in Paul: in 1 Cor. 6.9, θεοῦ βασιλείαν (with κληρονομεῖν in the future tense); in 6.10, βασιλείαν θεοῦ (with the same verb form); in 15.50, βασιλείαν θεοῦ (with κληρονομῆσαι); in Gal. 5.21, βασιλείαν θεοῦ (with the same verb form as 1 Cor. 6.9); in Eph. 5.5, κληρονομίαν ἐν τῇ βασιλείᾳ τοῦ Χριστοῦ καὶ Θεοῦ.[3] In addition, 1 Cor. 15.24, 1 Thess. 2.12, and

---

[1] E. Schweizer, 'Πνεῦμα', III, 1, d.

[2] Behm, ''Αρραβών', in Kittel, BAND I, p. 474. For the same conclusion, see: K. Deissner, *Auferstehungshoffnung und Pneumagedanke bei Paulus*, p. 69; Vas, op. cit., p. 73; Sokolowski, *Die Begriffe Geist und Leben bei Paulus*, p. 95; and Gunkel, *Die Wirkungen des heiligen Geistes*, p. 63.

[1] 'Κληρονόμος is, according to what had been said, an eschatological concept. . . . The kingdom, the inheritance is the new world in which God alone and completely rules. . . . Since Paul can look upon this as future, Rom. 8.23, so, only more

2 Thess. 1.5 all definitely relate the kingdom to the future. Eph. 5.5 introduces the question what significance (if any), lies in the distinction between God's kingdom and Christ's kingdom? The answer throws the primarily future nature of God's kingdom into even sharper relief. Col. 1.13 makes it clear that the redeemed and forgiven are now already placed (μετέστησεν, aorist, 'has transferred') in Christ's kingdom βασιλείαν τοῦ υἱοῦ τῆς ἀγάπης αὐτοῦ, i.e. the Father's). This kingdom of the Son's is the present kingdom, and, according to 1 Cor. 15.24, it will be replaced 'at the end' by the Father's kingdom (εἶτα τὸ τέλος, ὅταν παραδιδοῖ τὴν βασιλείαν). This primarily future character of the kingdom of God in Paul as distinguished from the present kingdom of Christ is recognised by Professor Cullmann.[1]

Now we turn to the relation between the kingdom of God and the Spirit affirmed in Rom. 14.17: 'but the kingdom of God is (ἐστιν) righteousness, and peace and joy in the Holy Spirit' (ἐν πνεύματι ἁγίῳ).[2] This means that the Spirit is the vital principle of the kingdom which produces the effects in human life that are appropriate to future life in the kingdom.[3] Added to the Spirit, ἁγίῳ here emphasises the uniqueness of the Spirit

exclusively, is κληρονομία to the Christian a thing to be hoped for.' Foerster, 'Κληρονόμος', in Kittel, BAND III, p. 782.

Michaelis remarks: 'In addition to the passages already mentioned (Gal. 5.21, 1 Cor. 6.5, 10, Eph. 5.5,) further word about inheriting the kingdom of God is 1 Cor. 15.20: from this passage it is quite definite that the kingdom of God will begin only after the resurrection of the dead.' Michaelis' general conclusion is that 'for Paul also the kingdom of God is still the eschatological entity that it was for the Baptist and for Jesus'. *Reich Gottes und Geist Gottes nach dem Neuen Testament*, p. 41, n. 54.

'Then πνεῦμα and κληρονομία belong together; one is the present, the other the future partaking of Christians in the Kingdom of God.' Gunkel, *Die Wirkungen des heiligen Geistes*, p. 64.

[1] 'The endless discussion over the question whether the kingdom of God in the New Testament is present or future would perhaps have taken another turn if one had simply made the definitely present, temporal differentiation between the βασιλεία τοῦ υἱοῦ . . . and the βασιλεία τοῦ θεοῦ. . . . In 1 Cor. 15.23ff the Son, to whom the Father has subjected all things, will subject Himself to the Father and give the rule over to the Father only after His return and the accompanying events. . . . Only then will the time of the new creation, of the kingdom of God the Father, be there.' (The same conclusion is drawn from a consideration of Col. 1.13.) Cullmann, *Koenigsherrschaft Christi und Kirche im Neuen Testament*, pp. 11-12.

[2] 'There is no reason here, as many assume for contesting the eschatological character of the idea of the kingdom.' E. Gaugler, *Der Römerbrief, Prophezei*, I, p. 350.

[3] 'The causal ἐν πνεύμα τι ἁγίω belongs not only to χαρά but to everything which renews the believing. Righteousness and peace also arise through the Holy Spirit', A. Schlatter, *Gottes Gerechtigkeit*, p. 376. Gunkel, *Die Wirkungen des heiligen Geistes*, p. 63, recognises the appropriateness of the Spirit to the kingdom. 'There must exist then an inner connexion in Paul between the concepts: πνεῦμα and βασιλεία τοῦ θεοῦ.'

appropriate to the uniqueness of the kingdom as God's kingdom. In our context this has the effect of making more definite the linking of the Spirit with the kingdom. Thus we may conclude that this connexion of the Spirit with the kingdom of God further proves our point that the Spirit belongs primarily to the future age. 1 Cor. 4.20 is an exact parallel to Rom. 14.17, carrying the same thought, but replacing an explicit reference to the Spirit with the concept δύναμις which (as we saw in Part 7 of the last chapter) implies the Spirit. Having shown that in Paul's eschatology the Spirit belongs primarily to the future, we must now glance at that eschatology in order to prevent several erroneous conclusions that might otherwise be drawn.

Without any further consideration one might be tempted to conclude, from Paul's future use of the kingdom of God, that Paul's eschatology was oriented solely toward the future. For in Acts the whole content of his missionary teaching and preaching is described by the concept of the kingdom of God (Acts 19.8, 20.25, 28.23, 30). If this were the case, then Paul would be in sharp contrast with the Synoptic *Gospels*, in which the kingdom of God plays such a large role. For in them the kingdom is not only future but also present. W. G. Kuemmel has shown this conclusively.[1] The future kingdom was already at work in the person of Jesus. This distinguished the eschatology of the early Church from the Jewish eschatology of the time.[2] But if, as is the case with Paul, the Lord has ascended and the kingdom of God is still primarily a future reality, what prevents Paul from falling back into a Jewish concentration on the future while living in an empty present? The answer is found in his doctrine of the Spirit. Just as in the Synoptics the future kingdom breaks into the present in the action of Jesus, so in Paul the future age has broken into the present in the action of the Spirit. The role of the Spirit in Paul's teaching is similar to that of the kingdom in

[1] 'This eschatological character of the present obtains with Jesus its full meaning, however, only through the numerous sayings in which Jesus sees the reign of God itself already realised in the present in His person, His action, and His preaching. For these sayings about the present are no chance utterances, but give the key to Jesus' preaching about the future: because in Jesus Himself the coming bringer of the reign of God has appeared in the present; because in Him the powers of the coming aeon were already at work; . . . for this reason the connexion with the man Jesus means the connexion with the coming reign of God which already is at work in a preliminary way in the present.' Kuemmel, *Verheissung und Erfüllung*, pp. 145-6.
[2] 'Early Christianity, like late Judaism, also knows the expectation of the coming kingdom; however it knows about more; it sees itself drawn into the incomprehensible power of this kingdom.' Preisker, *Geist und Leben*, p. 16.

the Synoptics. In the Synoptics, 'kingdom' denotes the situation in which God rules; in Paul, 'the Spirit' defines the same situation in terms of the inner dynamic which implements God's rule.[1] This will become evident when, in the next chapter, the present action of the Spirit is interpreted in the light of the first two. Paul's doctrine of the Spirit should throw as much light on his eschatology as the study of the Kingdom has thrown on the eschatology of the Synoptics. If this should prove to be the case, it is truly amazing that no one has yet taken full cognisance of this fact in the study of Paul.

Apart from the doctrine of the Spirit, this break-in of the future into the present agrees with Paul's use of other eschatological terms. Paul describes the present time as 'this age' ($\acute{o}$ $\alpha\grave{\iota}\grave{\omega}\nu$ $o\tilde{\upsilon}\tau os$: Rom. 12.2, 1 Cor. 1.20, 2.6, 3.18, 2 Cor. 4.4), and once as 'the present evil age' ($\acute{o}$ $\alpha\grave{\iota}\grave{\omega}\nu$ $\acute{o}$ $\acute{\epsilon}\nu\epsilon\sigma\tau\grave{\omega}s$ $\pi o\nu\eta\rho\acute{o}s$, Gal. 1.4). That 'this age' is not the blessed age to come is clear from $\pi o\nu\eta\rho\acute{o}s$, which 'is characteristic for the manner in which Paul speaks of the present aeon as the aeon of sin'.[2] Once the future age is specifically mentioned as the age to come ($o\grave{\upsilon}$ $\mu\acute{o}\nu o\nu$ $\acute{\epsilon}\nu$ $\tau\tilde{\omega}$ $\alpha\grave{\iota}\tilde{\omega}\nu\iota$ $\tau o\acute{\upsilon}\tau\omega$ $\grave{\alpha}\lambda\lambda\grave{\alpha}$ $\kappa\alpha\grave{\iota}$ $\acute{\epsilon}\nu$ $\tau\tilde{\omega}$ $\mu\acute{\epsilon}\lambda\lambda o\nu\tau\iota$, Eph. 1.21), which makes it clear that the future is still outstanding. But nevertheless something decisive has already taken place. For in 1 Cor. 10.11 Christians are described as those 'upon whom the end of the ages ($\tau\grave{\alpha}$ $\tau\acute{\epsilon}\lambda\eta$ $\tau\tilde{\omega}\nu$ $\alpha\grave{\iota}\acute{\omega}\nu\omega\nu$) has come'. In view of the eschatological meaning of $\tau\acute{\epsilon}\lambda os$, Sasse objects to the interpretation of J. Weiss and Lietzmann that here it is meant that the old age has passed and the coming age has begun.[3] But it is precisely this 'eschatological meaning' which leads us to follow Weiss and Lietzmann, providing it be understood that 'the end' can be in a real sense present for Christians (Paul is here addressing 'the church of God which is at Corinth') without time having run its full course to the appointed end. Only our understanding of the present as the time in which for Christians the future age is breaking-in in the Spirit gives meaning to Paul's concept of the interplay of present and future. Thus a glance at Paul's

[1] It might well be that Luke's description of Paul's message in terms of the Kingdom is a case of his interpreting Paul's activities with categories of his own theology—which was of course all he could do. This would then explain why Paul uses 'Kingdom' so infrequently in his writings, although it is so widely attributed to him by Luke.

[2] Compare 2 Cor. 4.4 and 1 Cor. 2.6. Sasse, '$\alpha\grave{\iota}\acute{\omega}\nu$', in Kittel, BAND I, p. 205.

[3] Weiss, *Der erste Korintherbrief*, p. 254; Lietzmann, *An die Korinther I/II*, p. 47; Sasse, op. cit., p. 203.

eschatological terminology shows that the interrelation of future and present which we shall consider in the next chapter is in agreement with the whole context of his thought about the Holy Spirit and time.

III

THE SPIRIT AND THE ESCHATOLOGICAL TENSION OF CHRISTIAN LIFE

IN Ch. I it was shown that the Spirit is the Spirit of Christ. Christologically, the function of the Spirit is to reveal Christ to man, bind the believer to Christ, and impart to His own the risen Christ's life of resurrection and exaltation. This ties the work of the Spirit to the redemptive acts of God in Christ in the past. In Ch. II, however, we have just seen that the Spirit belongs primarily to the future, in the sense that what we witness of the post-resurrection action of the Spirit can be understood only when viewed as a breaking-in of the future into the present. In other words, on the basis of the work of Christ, the power of the redeemed future has been released to act in the present in the person of the Holy Spirit.[1] By describing the Spirit as the power of the redeemed future we do not thereby make the Spirit any less the Spirit of Christ. The redeemed future is defined Christologically. It is the time of the consummated Lordship of Christ when He shall have 'put all his enemies under his feet' (1 Cor. 15.25). The point is simply that in order to understand Paul's doctrine of the Spirit we must consider it both Christologically and eschatologically.

The task of this third chapter is to bring this Christological and eschatological understanding of Spirit to bear on the present. In so doing we should accomplish two things. First we should find confirmation of the points already made in Chs. I and II. And secondly, we should throw new light on our understanding of the life of the believer.

There is a definite reason why an understanding of the Spirit leads to an understanding of Christian life in the present. The Spirit bridges the dialectic of the believer's situation. As Professor Cullmann has pointed out, the dialectic and dualism of the New Testament is the dialectic of present and future, or of already fulfilled and not yet fulfilled, or of possessed and

---

[1] 'However, in the midst of this world the powers of the future world already show themselves', Gunkel, *Die Wirkungen des heiligen Geistes*, p. 64.

promised.[1] As we have seen, the Spirit belongs primarily to the future, the not-yet-fulfilled, the promised. And, at the same time (as was implicit in Ch. I and will become explicit in this chapter), the Spirit is given now; He is present; He is already possessed. Therefore, through the study of the workings of the Spirit, we shall be able to pick out the elements of 'already' and 'not yet' in Christian life better, perhaps, than we can from any other point of view. This should not be interpreted to mean that each operation of the Spirit should be assigned to an 'already' column or a 'not yet' column. Rather it will usually be the case that an already-fulfilling operation of the Spirit also implies a not-yet-fulfilled aspect of that same operation of the Spirit. This will become clearer in the consideration of concrete cases.

1. *The Spirit in the Present*

By way of complement and contrast to the fact that the Spirit belongs primarily to the future, we find the Spirit very much in the present to Paul and his fellow Christians. This comes most clearly to expression in the two passages which refer to the κοινωνία of the Spirit—namely 2 Cor. 13.13 and Phil. 2.2.[2] Underlying both passages is the assumption that this κοινωνία is for every Christian (μετὰ πάντων ὑμῶν, 2 Cor. 13.13),[3] not just for a select few. In both verses κοινωνία is accompanied by the genitive πνεύματος. In 2 Cor. 13.13 the first two phrases refer to a person and his gift, but in the third phrase (according to Hauck)[4] only the gift is mentioned. The proper parallel members would then be: 'grace, love, Spirit' (not 'Christ, God, Spirit'). But Hauck fails to take into account the possibility that the Spirit could be both a gift and a giver, a possibility which Windisch's analysis leaves open.[5] This reading is strengthened by the parallel of Phil. 2.1 which, according to Lohmeyer, is introduced by a similar three-phrase clause in which Christ, love, and Spirit are parallel.[6] Here Spirit could be a subject like

---

[1] Cullmann, *Christ and Time*, p. 146, 'the only dialectic and the only dualism that is found in the New Testament . . . is not the dialectic between this world and the Beyond; moreover, it is not that between time and eternity; it is rather the dialectic of present and future.'

[2] The verse designated as *v.* 13 according to German usage is designated as *v.* 14 in the Revised Standard Version. Nestle labels it 13.

[3] Gunkel, *Die Wirkungen des heiligen Geistes*, p. 96.

[4] Hauck, 'Κοινωνία', in Kittel, BAND III, p. 804.

[5] Windisch, *Der Zweite Korintherbrief*, p. 428.

[6] Lohmeyer, *Die Briefe an die Philipper, an die Kolosser und an Philemon*, p. 82.

Christ. Thus our translation of κοινωνία in both cases ought to include both the ideas of fellowship with the Spirit as well as participation in His gifts. Since 'fellowship' includes 'participation', it is the best translation.[1] The point for our discussion is that in both these passages we have asserted the presence of the Spirit to the believer now as really and as importantly as the presence of the grace of Christ and the presence of the love of God.

Eph. 1.13 also presents the relation of the Spirit to the believer in such a way that we see the Spirit as present to the believer not only now while he believes in Christ, but also after the time when the believer takes possession of his inheritance in the future age. Here we have a function of the Spirit in the believer's present which is only meaningful in relation to the future. Those who believed in Christ were sealed (ἐσφραγίσθητε) with the promised Holy Spirit. Now σφραγίζειν means two things.[2] First it is a mark of recognition—in this case, to mark those who are in Christ (ἐν ᾧ) (compare Ezek. 9.4ff). The implication is that the Spirit is present to all those who are Christ's. Precisely the same idea is stated negatively in Rom. 8.9. Secondly, there is the idea of equipping with heavenly power (John 6.27) in view of an eschatological end, which leads into the ἀρραβών and κληρονομία of v. 14. Because this only happens in 'Christ' we trace the Christocentric as well as the eschatological element in the presence of the Spirit. The believer is already sealed, but his inheritance is not yet possessed.[3] Eph. 4.30 relates the Spirit's sealing to the end. Christians have been sealed 'for the day of redemption' (εἰς ἡμέραν ἀπολυτρώσεως).

But the presence of the Spirit is most evident in that the Spirit dwells (οἰκεῖν) in the believer. This 'dwelling' designates the Spirit's rule over the believer, and a continuous union with him.[4] As such the Spirit 'inhabits', 'lives' in the Church

[1] Contrary to Hauck, who prefers 'participation in' in both instances in exclusion of fellowship. Lietzmann, *Korinther I/II*, p. 162, reads 'fellowship' in 2 Cor. 13.13, and Dibelius, *An die Philipper*, reads 'fellowship' in Phil. 2.1.

[2] Reinhard, *Das Wirken des heiligen Geistes im Menschen nach dem Briefen des Apostels Paulus*, pp. 20, 21.

[3] Bauer, *Griechisch-Deutsches Wörterbuch*, p. 1447. Another eschatological element comes from the past. The 'promised' Holy Spirit refers to the Spirit in the present as an element of the future promised in the Old Testament, especially to Abraham (Gal. 3.14). Gunkel, *Die Wirkungen des heiligen Geistes*, p. 62, and Sokolowski, *Die Begriffe Geist und Leben bei Paulus*, p. 95, recognise the eschatological element in sealing.

[4] Michel, 'Οἰκέω', in Kittel, BAND V, pp. 137-8.

28

(1 Cor. 3.16, Eph. 2.22) as well as in the individual (Rom. 8.9, 11). This indwelling of the Spirit is Christocentric in that it is equivalent to Christ in the believer (Rom. 8.9, 10). Eschatologically, the future resurrection (Rom. 8.11), sonship which involves a right to future inheritance (8.15-17) and redemption of the body at the new creation (8.23) all are based on this 'dwelling' in the present. This habitation of the Spirit provides continuously a sphere of life and action (8.9 'in the Spirit') which replaces the unredeemed, natural 'in the flesh' (ibid.).[1] The permanence of this indwelling is emphasised by the companion concepts of 'temple' and 'dwelling place', 'lodging' (κατοικητήριον: 1 Cor. 3.16, Eph. 2.22).[2] As further evidence of the presence of the Spirit to the believer, we discover that Christian life as a whole flows from the working of the Spirit.

2. *The Spirit and the Christian's life as a whole*

According to Paul, as Gunkel saw, 'the whole life of the Christian is an effect of the πνεῦμα'.[3] In Rom. 8.9 he describes the life of the believer as being 'in the Spirit' (ἐν πνεύματι). In Rom. 7.6 he uses a similar expression, 'in the new life of the Spirit' (ἐν καινότητι πνεύματος), and in 1 Cor. 12.3 he uses ἐν πνεύματι twice. This phrase means being the subject of a special action of the Spirit.[4] He who is ἐν πνεύματι becomes the organ through which the Spirit expresses Himself, just as in 1 Cor. 12.3, where the speaking of the Christian is attributed to the Spirit. This being in the Spirit is the same kind of phenomenon as the case of a man possessed by an evil spirit (Mark 1.23, 5.2), in which case Jesus addresses the spirit rather than the man, since the man is determined by the spirit.[5] This total submission of life to the Spirit is illuminated by the former status ἐν σαρκί (Rom. 8.9), which it replaces. 'In the flesh' means 'under the domination of the flesh', and for Paul describes the total situation of the non-Christian.[6] And so the total domination of the Spirit replaces the total domination of the flesh. Again the Christo-

---

[1] This whole line of thought of the contrast of σάρξ and πνεῦμα which reappears continually in Paul is further evidence of the steady working of the Spirit in the present.

[2] Dibelius, *An die Kolosser, Epheser, an Philemon*, p. 72, translates κατοικητήριον, 'Behausung'.

[3] Gunkel, *Die Wirkungen des heiligen Geistes*, p. 75.

[4] Bauer, *Griechisch-Deutsches Wörterbuch*, p. 470.

[5] Gunkel, op. cit., p. 36.

[6] Sanday and Headlam, *The Epistle to the Romans*, p. 196, and note on σάρξ and πνεῦμα, p 181.

logical and eschatological combine in the action of the Spirit, for Rom. 8.10 equates Christ in the believer with being in the Spirit. And in Gal. 5.25, Paul expresses the same thought as ἐν πνεύματι by means of the simple instrumental dative πνεύματι.[1]

The usage 'the law of the Spirit' (ὁ νόμος τοῦ πνεύματος, Rom. 8.2) is also equivalent to the subjection of the whole of Christian life in the present to the Spirit. Here νόμος does not have its proper meaning of a code which prescribes action according to set regulations. Rather the Spirit replaces the function of such a code and by His determining influences produces regulated action without any code.[2] In harmony with this replacing of the Law, the Spirit takes over the former functions of the Law as the norm and guide for all of life. Consequently Christians are to 'walk according to the Spirit' (περιπατοῦσιν . . . κατὰ πνεῦμα, Rom. 8.4), or 'walk by the Spirit' (πνεύματι περιπατεῖτε, Gal. 5.16; πνεύματι . . . στοιχῶμεν, Gal. 5.25). As Preisker points out, with reservations, it is the particular service of Paul often to have succeeded in the attempt to relate questions of life to the basics of Christian faith rather than treating them at the level of morality.[3] This is especially evident in Gal. 5.25, where the conduct of life is measured by the source of redemptive life, i.e. the Spirit. Paul uses περιπατεῖν exclusively in the figurative sense, and it means 'to live', 'to conduct one's self'[4]; while στοιχεῖν adds the idea of a standard for life and conduct.[5] Here in Gal. 5.25 it should be translated 'to walk (in a straight line)', 'to conduct one's self (rightly)'.[6] Gal. 5.18 expresses the same idea of the Spirit as the source of life (ἐν πνεύματι) *plus* the emphasis of the Spirit as the norm of conduct (κατὰ πνεῦμα), by means of the phrase 'led by the Spirit' (πνεύματι ἄγεσθε). Corresponding to this drawing of all life under the sway of the Spirit, the attention, thought, affection, and will (φρόνημα) are all centred on the Spirit (Rom. 8.5, 6).[7] These texts are enough to show that the present life of the Christian is determined by the Spirit. Thus in the last analysis the Christian should be spiritual (πνευματικός: 1 Cor. 2.15, 3.1

---

[1] Schlier, '῾Ελεύθερος—Der Begriff der Freiheit im NT', in Kittel, BAND II, p. 197.
[2] Sanday and Headlam, op. cit., p. 190. Lietzmann, *An die Römer*, p. 78.
[3] Preisker, *Geist und Leben*, p. 167.
[4] Burton, *The Epistle to the Galatians*, p. 298.
[5] This is a technical military term meaning 'to arrange one's self in the proper order' (probably related to our command, 'Fall in'). Schlier, op. cit., p. 197 n.
[6] Burton, op. cit., p. 322.
[7] Burton, op. cit., p. 195.

14.37). But the nature of the Christian life in the present can only be understood with reference to the future precisely because it is the work of the Spirit. This will become evident in a consideration of particular aspects of Christian life which show clearly the definitive orientation to the future of all operations of the Spirit.

3. The Spirit and the present tension: sonship, faith, hope, love, prayer, and glorification

In Gal. 3 and 4 Paul introduces the subject of the sonship of the believer, founding it on the work of Christ (the Christocentric factor), and at the same time associating it with the Spirit. In Gal. 3.14, he equates the blessing promised to Abraham's offspring with the Spirit,[1] who comes upon the Gentiles because of Christ (ἐν Ἰησοῦ Χριστῷ, 'by virtue of being in Christ').[2] And again in 3.26 with the parallel phrase (ἐν Χριστῷ Ἰησοῦ) sonship is based on Christ. In Gal. 4.6, 7, he relates sonship to both Christ and the Spirit. The Spirit is the mark of the believer's sonship because it designates sonship generally, as we saw in Rom. 1.4, where the Spirit was the means of designating Jesus Son of God. Therefore the Spirit is here the 'Spirit of His son' (τὸ πνεῦμα τοῦ υἱοῦ). And since believers are 'in Christ' they share sonship with Him, and with that sonship its distinguishing mark, the Spirit. The Spirit provides subjective evidence (εἰς τὰς καρδίας ἡμῶν) to the believer of his objective sonship. This comes to concrete expression in the cry, Ἀββά, ὁ πατήρ, which was probably in common usage, the Aramaic being traceable to Jesus.[3] Since in Gal. 3.1-5 the receipt of the Spirit is spoken of implicitly as the sum of the benefits of Christ's redemption, and since sonship seems to be the grounds for sending the Spirit (ὅτι δέ ἐστι υἱοί, 'and because you are sons'),[4] a believer's sonship would be questionable without this cry in the heart.

The eschatological aspects of sonship appear only however when we turn to Rom. 8. In v. 14 Paul equates being led by the Spirit with sonship. Therefore in v. 15 it is appropriate for him to describe the Spirit as 'the Spirit of sonship' (πνεῦμα υἱοθεσίας); that is to say, the Spirit is appropriate to the status

[1] Burton, op. cit., p. 176.   [2] Burton, op. cit., p. 124.
[3] Burton, op. cit., p. 224.
[4] Burton, op. cit., p. 221, Schlier, op. cit., p. 139.

of sonship, presumably, on the basis of the general proposition of $v.$ 14.[1] As the Spirit of sonship, then, the Spirit bears witness to the believer's sonship by means of the cry, Ἀββὰ, ὁ πατήρ. So far the situation is the same as in Gal. 4.6. Through this witness the Spirit provides the believer with the subjective certainty of his sonship. This is the already-fulfilled, present function of the Spirit in relation to sonship. But sonship has a not-yet-fulfilled, future aspect.

The status of sonship relates believers to God as His children (τέκνα Θεοῦ, $v.$ 16) and the right of inheritance follows. Believers are also heirs of God (κληρονόμοι . . . Θεοῦ, $v.$ 17). The inheritance to be received is defined with respect to Christ. Because heirs of God are fellow heirs of Christ (συγκληρονόμοι . . . Χριστοῦ, $v.$ 17) they will receive what He received, i.e. they will be glorified with Him (συνδοξασθῶμεν, $v.$ 17), will have the future glory (μέλλουσαν δόξαν) revealed in them as it has already been revealed in Christ ($v.$ 18). With this future aspect of sonship still to be fulfilled, Paul describes the leading of the Spirit in the present and the witness of the Spirit in the present as merely first-fruits which the Spirit gives of the complete sonship (τὴν ἀπαρχὴν τοῦ πνεύματος, $v.$ 23).[2] $V.$ 23, then, is a summary of the whole preceding section of Rom. 8. The indwelling, freeing, normative, leading, witnessing actions of the Spirit are only first-fruits in the present of the complete action of the Spirit in the future. In relation to sonship specifically, believers wait eagerly for (ἀπεκδεχόμενοι) adoption which is further defined as the redemption of the body (τὴν ἀπολύτρωσιν τοῦ σώματος, $v.$ 23). This future redemption of the body is the not-yet-fulfilled, the future aspect of sonship which the Spirit will fulfil. That it is a function of the Spirit is clear from $v.$ 11. Thus in the case of sonship the Spirit's action in the present is merely preliminary. The Spirit's properly completed work lies in the future.

A further aspect of Christian life which illustrates this tension

---

[1] Michel, Der Brief an die Römer, p. 167.

[2] It is interesting to note that ἀπαρχὴν τοῦ πνεύματος has been generally interpreted as a genitive of apposition. Even Nygren, Commentary on Romans, p. 333, who sees most clearly the tension between future and present in this chapter, constricts the meaning of this phrase. Gaugler, Der Römerbrief, Prophezei, 1, p. 309, may interpret it broadly, but he is not specific at this point. Michel, op. cit., p. 176, n. 1, correctly rejects the possibility of the phrase meaning a partial outpouring of the Spirit in the present. The best interpretation seems to me to be: 'we ourselves, who have the first-fruits of what the Spirit has to give, wait for the full working of the Spirit, i.e. adoption as sons, the redemption of our bodies.'

of already and not yet is faith. By 'faith', in this particular instance, we mean faith in the sense of a sure confidence in God's promises concerning the future. This meaning of 'faith' is most explicit in 2 Cor. 5.7, where the present is the visible and the future, the invisible. To walk in relation to the invisible future takes faith.[1] In 2 Cor. 4.13 and Gal. 5.5 Paul relates this idea of faith to the Spirit. In 2 Cor. 4.13* he speaks of 'the same Spirit of faith' (τὸ αὐτὸ πνεῦμα τῆς πίστεως) where τὸ αὐτὸ refers to the same Spirit that moved the psalmist who wrote the passage (Ps. 116.10) which Paul cites. That πίστεως here refers to a reliance on the future fulfilment of a promise is clear from the following verse, in which the expected fulfilment is resurrection and entrance into the presence of God.[2] This faith or confidence with regard to the future expresses itself in the present in Paul's case in the speaking (λαλοῦμεν), witnessing, preaching of his apostolic ministry. The 'Spirit of faith' means 'the Spirit which produces such faith'. The same Spirit produced the same faith both in the psalmist and in Paul.[3] Why should it be the Spirit which produces this faith? Because it is the Spirit which bridges the gap between present and future. Paul is confident that he has (ἔχοντες) the Spirit in the present. But because the Spirit was the resurrection power of Christ and will also effect Paul's resurrection, Paul may carry out his ministry in a mood of security in reliance on the future. The already-fulfilled aspect of the Spirit's work is a confidence which enables one to 'speak'. The not-yet-fulfilled work of the Spirit is the resurrection. In this analysis of faith, a primary reference of the Spirit to the future is seen to determine the understanding of the present possession of the Spirit. The confidence in the present is only possible in the light of the future.

The same operation of the Spirit in relation to this meaning of faith is even more evident in Gal. 5.5. 'Out of faith with regard to the Spirit, we wait for the hoped for righteousness.' Earlier in the same letter (3.2) Paul makes the Galatians' receipt of the Spirit the distinguishing mark of their Christianity over against their earlier Judaism. Thus in 5.5 the present working of the Spirit is assumed to be common knowledge among the

---

[1] For this meaning of faith see: Bauer, *Griechisch-Deutsches Wörterbuch*, p. 1208 (2d.β), Sanday and Headlam, *The Epistle to the Romans*, p. 33 (iii).
[2] Lietzmann here agrees with Kuemmel, *Verheissung und Erfüllung*, p. 116.
[3] Windisch, *Der Zweite Korintherbrief*, p. 148, suggests this as one alternative but prefers another.

Galatians, and will a few verses later provide the whole basis for the Christian life. By means of, or out of regard to, this present working of the Spirit ($\pi\nu\epsilon\acute{u}\mu\alpha\tau\iota$), a faith arises which produces, or out of which comes ($\dot{\epsilon}\kappa$ $\pi\acute{\iota}\sigma\tau\epsilon\omega\varsigma$), an expectation concerning the future.[1] In this case what is expected in the future is a righteousness ($\dot{\epsilon}\lambda\pi\acute{\iota}\delta\alpha$ $\delta\iota\kappa\alpha\iota\sigma\sigma\acute{u}\nu\eta\varsigma$).[2] Does the Spirit play a role in this future righteousness? With regard to the present waiting of the believer 'by the Spirit' is an instrumental dative. The Spirit enables the believer to wait in a way appropriate to the future righteous. ('Wait by the Spirit' parallels 'walk by the Spirit', v. 16; 'led by the Spirit', v. 18; and 'live by the Spirit', v. 25). That one's relation to the Spirit in the present somehow conditions one's standing with God in the future is clear from 5.21 and 6.8. By $\delta\iota\kappa\alpha\iota\sigma\sigma\acute{u}\nu\eta\varsigma$ Paul means the final acceptance of God at the end after which there is no possibility of rejection. But, and this is the point, if the present life, the present waiting of the believer, is not determined by and grounded in the Spirit, that final decision of God may be rejection. And to prevent any thought of any kind of self-righteousness the following verse (v. 6) reminds us that this Spirit-life is only available 'in Christ Jesus'. Again the present and future aspects of the Spirit are present. In the present the believer has confidence about his final acceptance in the future because his present life of waiting is already grounded in the same Spirit which will so continue to determine his life until the end that he will be finally accepted as righteous. In the same chapter, v. 4 implies that the man who waits 'by the Spirit' is for that reason for the present in grace, justified, righteous. And out of faith in that Spirit he may expect to be judged righteous at the end of the age.

Since the present work of the Spirit is understood by Paul as a breaking-in of the powers of the future, we would expect that

[1] *Πνεύματι* is a combination of an instrumental dative and a dative of respect. It is an instrumental dative with regard to ἀπεδεχόμεθα, for as Burton, *The Epistle to the Galatians*, p. 273, points out, in πνεύματι and ἐκ πίστεως we have a succession of co-ordinate limitation similar to Rom. 3.25. That they are not merely co-ordinate is clear from their difference of construction which suggests a relation between them. And here I suggest that with relation to ἐκ πίστεως, πνεύματι is a dative of respect in that it is true that the believer may have faith in view of the action of the Spirit. The thought then in regard to faith is: in view of the present activity of the Spirit the believer had a confidence with regard to the future which produces an expectant waiting.

[2] *Δικαιοσύνης* is an objective genitive thus: 'hoped-for righteousness'. It is the object of both hope and expectation. Burton, op. cit., p. 279. Also Schlier, *Der Brief an die Galater*, p. 168.

34

the work of the Spirit would inspire hope. The shade of difference here between faith and hope is that faith is directed to
the God who promises, while hope is directed more to the
promises themselves. In Rom. 15.13 hope is based on the Spirit.
Paul wishes the Roman Christians joy and peace in their belief
in order that they may abound in hope (εἰς τὸ περισσεύειν ὑμᾶς
ἐν τῇ ἐλπίδι). But this overflow of hope is ἐν δυνάμει πνεύματος
ἁγίου. That ἐν τῇ ἐλπίδι is the object of εἰς τὸ περισσεύειν is clear
from the phrase which introduces the verse and its main point—
ὁ θεὸς τῆς ἐλπίδος. Then ἐν δυνάμει κτλ is the ground of this
abounding in hope. How is it that Paul mentions the power of
the Spirit in connexion with God's hope? The thought is clear
when the Spirit is understood as primarily the power of the
future. On the basis of the Spirit's action in the present (δυνάμει
emphasises the Spirit in action), the believer may infer the
future is in a measure already here and thus be filled with hope
that the future age is no fiction and will surely come. Phil. 1. 19
shows how Paul relies on the equipment of the Spirit (ἐπιχορηγίας
τοῦ πνεύματος), when his death as a martyr is a possibility, just
because the Spirit belongs to the future and therefore is the
One who can conduct him into the future. The underlying
Christological foundation is clear.

Rom. 5.5 again bases hope on the action of the Spirit. In
this case the action of the Spirit is specified as the mediating of
God's love. The eternal nature of God's love (1 Cor. 13.8, 13),
as well as the eschatological nature of the Spirit's action in the
present, provides the ground of hope. The present aspect of
hope, then, is the Spirit-produced love of God. The same Spirit
gives the content to the thing hoped for. Rom. 5.2 defines the
hope as sharing the glory of God, and from 2 Cor. 3.4ff we have
already seen that the Spirit mediates that glory. Here again
in the work of the Spirit we have the already and not-yet aspects
represented: God's love in the present—glory in the future—
both supplied by the Spirit.

(It is interesting to note in the relation between God's love
and the Spirit that there are no eschatological elements which
may be separated into already, in the present, and not yet, in the
future. The reason is of course that God's love does not vary
with time.)

Prayer is another aspect of the Christian life in which the
Spirit's work in the present relates to a further work in the future.

In this case the future aspect is only implicit, and not expressly stated by Paul. In our considerations of Rom. 8.15 and Gal. 4.6 we have already seen that a particular prayer of the believer is both a witness of the Spirit and at the same time the prayer of the Spirit.[1] But Eph. 6.18 and Rom. 8.26, 27, relate all prayer to the Spirit. The necessity for praying in the Spirit (ἐν πνεύματι, Eph. 6.18) is based on the believer's weakness (τῇ ἀσθενείᾳ, Rom. 8.26). This weakness consists in an inability to know what to say (τὸ γὰρ τί προσευξώμεθα;).[2] Corresponding to this weakness the Spirit stands by to help (συναντιλαμβάνεται) and in view of the loss of words, intercedes for the believer (ὑπερεντυγχάνει).[3] That this intercession of the Spirit is in inexpressible groans (στεναγμοὶ ἀλάλητοι) suggests that impossible-to-understand prayer called 'speaking in tongues'. That this expressly designated gift of the Spirit (1 Cor. 12.10) is prayer is clear from 1 Cor. 14.2, 14, 16, 17, 28. 1 Corinthians describes the content of speaking in tongues as 'uttering mysteries in the Spirit' (πνεύματι δὲ λαλεῖ μυστήρια). At this point one could already conclude simply from the eschatological nature of the Spirit,[4] that distinctively Christian prayer, i.e. prayer in the Spirit, is an eschatological phenomenon. But the purpose of this chapter is not only to throw light on the eschatological nature of some of the aspects of the Christian life but also to further support the thesis (Ch. II) that the Spirit belongs primarily to the future. And as a matter of fact we find in the present action of the Spirit in prayer the suggestion of a further corresponding action in the future.

Both the terms which describe the content of prayer in the Spirit have an eschatological nuance. The sighs or groans (στεναγμοὶ) of Rom. 8.26 recall the same word in verb form in vv. 22 and 23. In both cases it is a groaning after, or sighing for, an eschatological fulfilment still outstanding. The mysteries (μυστήρια) of 1 Cor. 14.2 suggest a future unveiling, for it belongs to the nature of mysteries that they be sometime revealed (Rom. 16.25, 26; Col. 1.27; Eph. 3.8, 9).[5] With these threads

[1] Bieder, *Gebetswirklichkeit und Gebetsmoeglichkeit bei Paulus*, sees in these passages the ground of the possibility of prayer in the Spirit's teaching us to address God as Father. [2] Sanday and Headlam, *The Epistle to the Romans*, p. 213.
[3] Michel, *Der Brief an die Römer*, p. 177. Lietzmann, *An die Römer*, p. 87.
[4] Greeven, *Gebet und Eschatologie im Neuen Testament*, pp. 150, 161-2. Bieder, op. cit., p. 30.
[5] For this eschatological colouring of μυστήριον see Gunther Bornkamm, 'Μυστήριον', in Kittel, BAND IV, p. 829.

of thought out of the future, together with our knowledge of the Spirit nature of the future age, we are invited to conclude that the Spirit will be in the future, as well as in the present, the agent or medium of communication between God and man. The generalisation of Eph. 2.18 that access (προσαγωγὴν) to the Father is in the Spirit (ἐν ἑνὶ πνεύματι) lends weight to this conclusion. Thus the action of the Spirit in the present is evident in our opportunity and ability to pray. But in this communication with the Father the believer is himself in some measure left out (e.g., 1 Cor. 14.14, where the νοῦς does not participate). This privileged but imperfect present access in the Spirit looks forward to the time in the future when partial knowledge and weakness give way to a more perfect access to the Father in the same Spirit.

Finally, glorification of the individual exhibits the eschatological work of the Spirit in the present and the future. Glory (δόξα), like Spirit, carries a primarily eschatological meaning. When Paul speaks of the glorification of the believer it is with clear reference to the future (Rom. 5.2: 'We rejoice at the hope of the glory of God,' ἐπ' ἐλπίδι τῆς δόξης).[1] Eph. 3.16 shows that this glory is communicated already to the believer by means of the Spirit (διὰ τοῦ πνεύματος). The present benefit of this wealth of God's future glory (τὸ πλοῦτος τῆς δόξης) comes in the form of strengthening in power (δυνάμει κραταιωθῆναι) to the end (vv. 18, 19) that Christ's love may be comprehended and known. This present glorification of the believer in knowing Christ by means of the Spirit is again expressed in 2 Cor. 3.18. In reflecting (which includes beholding) the glory of the Lord (τὴν δόξαν κυρίου κατοπτριζόμενοι), the believer looks into the face of Christ (2 Cor. 4.6) and is glorified in the present (ἀπὸ δόξης). This same glorification will find its completion in the future (ἀπὸ δόξης εἰς δόξαν).[2] In both cases the Spirit is the agent of the glorification as is shown in the concluding mention of πνεύματος in apposition with κυρίου which echoes the thought of 3.17.[3]

Summary

For Paul, as we saw in Ch. II, the Spirit is primarily an

[1] See Rom. 8.17-18, 15.42-3, 2 Cor. 4.17, Phil. 3.21, 1 Thess. 2.12, 2 Thess. 2.14. For the same eschatology of glorification, see Kittel, 'Δόξα' in Kittel, BAND II, p. 253f.
[2] Windisch, Der Zweite Korintherbrief, p. 129.
[3] ibid.

eschatological entity. He is the power and life of the future. But instead of jumping to the mistaken conclusion that the Spirit's activity is confined to the future age, we have tried to show how decisively the Spirit is at work in the present. The Spirit of the future has been released into the present. This gracious, redemptive releasing of the Spirit into the present is based on the work of Christ and the benefits of the future are revealed to us primarily in the resurrected, exalted Lord. This point is founded in the conclusions of Ch. I, where it was shown how and in what sense the Spirit is the Spirit of Christ. This Christological foundation, then, provided the setting for our exposition of the presence of the Spirit for Christian life now.

In attempting to understand how the primarily eschatological Spirit is at work in the present one discovers the unique tension which characterises Christian life. This eschatological tension has definite implications for particular aspects of the believer's life.

In short we have tried to show that Paul's understanding of the Spirit is a Christological-eschatological one. The interpretation is confirmed by and at the same time illuminates Paul's idea of the life of the believer. In all of its essentials Paul's doctrine of the Spirit and eschatology has been developed.

In the next three chapters it remains to compare our results with current opinions in New Testament studies. But before doing so we are in a position now to draw some further, more generalised implications about the life of the believer and about the life of the Church.

In the final analysis, what is distinctive about the life of a Christian? Is the answer to be found in his attitudes and actions? Does the description of the varieties of his spiritual experiences help us? No, the tools of psychology are not adequate, for empirical methods can never discern what is distinctive. The attitudes and actions of any particular Christian may be disturbingly similar to those of a good pagan. The distinctive thing about a Christian must be sought outside of him. It is to be found in the source and goal of his life as a Christian. And from our investigations we can state with some assurance that the indwelling Spirit is the source of that life and the future consummation its goal. These two facts and their natural interconnexion account for all that is distinctive about the life of a Christian.

38

The presence of the Spirit in him has set the Christian apart from all unbelievers and from what he was himself before he believed. This is what makes him a saint, i.e. one set apart. The Christian is already sanctified (ἡγιάσθητε, 1 Cor. 6.11)—the thing has been done to him and for him as a work of the Spirit (ἐν τῷ πνεύματι, ibid.; ἡγιασμένη ἐν πνεύπατι ἁγίῳ, Rom. 15.16). [The Christian life is, then, first of all, a status granted to the believer.]

Secondly, it is a way of life. And in this sense the believer is still in the process of sanctification. His sanctification is something God wants of him which he must work out in an ethical holiness (1 Thess. 4.3, 7), but still on the basis of the fact that the Spirit has been given to him (1 Thess. 4.8). And why does the Spirit have a role in this active sanctification? Because the believer's way of life is the way to the new age whose principle is the Spirit (Rom. 14.17). His life is the same in kind as the life of the new age, but it is not yet consummated, for the consummation has not yet come. Meanwhile, realising with the Apostle that he is not yet perfected, he must press on toward the eschatological goal (Phil. 3.11-14), letting that new age realise itself in him in action appropriate to it (Gal. 5.22). This makes it clear why the Christian ethic cannot be derived from or defined by a set of principles. It takes its meaning from the new age (Rom. 14.17). It also shows why the attainment of 'perfection' in this life is impossible until the end comes and all is fulfilled. The believer never 'arrives', because the new age has not yet arrived. Thus the believer is not perfected, but his status and his life, in so far as they are determined by the Spirit, are of the same kind as his status and life will be after the consummation, and already he moves toward that goal.

What is true of the life of the individual Christian is also true of the life of the Church. The Church is a unique community by virtue of the indwelling of the Spirit (Eph. 2.19-22). That the Church is constituted by the presence of the Spirit is clear from the sacrament of initiation. In baptism the convert receives the Spirit and in so doing joins the Church, for in receiving the Spirit he shares what the fellowship has in common (1 Cor. 12.13).[1] The Spirit underlies the various activities of

---

[1] Where ἐβαπτίσθημεν and ἐποτίσθημεν express the same thought. The active agent in baptism is the Spirit, whom the convert is made to drink as though the Spirit were a fluid. The figure is no doubt suggested to Paul by the water at bap-

the Church at worship: in preaching and witnessing (1 Cor. 2.4, 13, 12.3; 1 Thess. 1.5); in listening (1 Thess. 1.7); in confession of faith (1 Cor. 12.3); in prayer (Rom. 8.26, 27; Eph. 6.18); and in singing (Eph. 5.18, 19). All the Spirit-inspired gifts of the individual members are only particular aspects of the total Spirit-life of the Church (1 Cor. 12.7ff, 14.12). The Church as the new Israel (Gal. 6.16) has a place in the eschatological scheme (Rom. 11.25, 26). Paul, however, subordinates the Church to the individual when speaking of the end, to avoid a repetition of the Jewish error of relying on membership in a fellowship as the decisive condition for salvation.

tism. Some indication of the Lord's Supper is also possible. Lietzmann, *An die Korinther I/II*, p. 63 and p. 188, for p. 63, line 24.

IV

ALBERT SCHWEITZER'S CONSISTENT ESCHATOLOGY

1. *Consistent Eschatology and the problem it addresses*

IN TURNING to Albert Schweitzer we come to the first of the great attempts in recent Biblical scholarship to understand the thought of the New Testament from an eschatological point of view. The term which Dr Schweitzer invented to designate his viewpoint is '*Konsequente Eschatologie*'. It is usually translated 'consistent eschatology', but appears as 'thoroughgoing eschatology' in W. Montgomery's translation of *Von Reimarus zu Wrede*.[1] No doubt Professor Dodd's label was modelled after Dr Schweitzer's and intended to indicate a contrast. Actually, no contrast is apparent in the terms themselves, since Dr Schweitzer's term describes a method of approaching an interpretation of New Testament thought, while Professor Dodd's term describes the kind of eschatological thought he finds in the New Testament. But, to be sure, behind the labels there are two sharply contrasting eschatological interpretations of the New Testament. In fact Dr Schweitzer finds in the New Testament and exalts to centrality just those elements of eschatology which Professor Dodd abhors and seeks to avoid. But we can best understand the significance of the term 'consistent eschatology' when we see it in the light of the problem to which Dr Schweitzer addresses himself and the method of attack which he uses in attempting to solve it.

The theological problem which Dr Schweitzer felt to be the paramount one was no doubt suggested to him by the efforts of Adolf Harnack. It is the problem of the history of dogma.

[1] The following abbreviations will be used in the footnotes to cite the English translations of Dr Schweitzer's works:
(a) *Quest* = *The Quest of the Historical Jesus*, London 1911. (English translation of *Von Reimarus zu Wrede*—now superseded by the later edition *Geschichte der Leben-Jesu-Forschung*.)
(b) *Interpreters* = *Paul and His Interpreters*, London 1912. (English translation of *Geschichte der Paulinischen Forschung*.)
(c) *Mysticism* = *The Mysticism of Paul the Apostle*, London 1953. (English translation of *Die Mystik des Apostels Paulus*.)

For all his appreciation of Harnack's *History of Dogma*, he feels that 'the solid mason-work only begins in the Greek period', and that 'what precedes is not placed on firm foundations but only supported on piles'.[1] The problem of the history of dogma remains for Dr Schweitzer, and his efforts are all an attempt to solve it. In his own words, 'the great and still undischarged task which confronts those engaged in the historical study of primitive Christianity is to explain how the teaching of Jesus developed into the early Greek theology, in the form in which it appears in the works of Ignatius, Justin, Tertullian, and Irenaeus. How could the doctrinal system of Paul arise on the basis of the life and work of Jesus and the beliefs of the primitive community; and how did the early Greek theology arise out of Paulinism?'[2]

To this problem Dr Schweitzer applies the method of scientific theology. 'The investigation of historical truth in itself I regard as the ideal for which scientific theology has to strive. I still hold fast to the opinion that the permanent spiritual importance that the religious thought of the past has for ours makes itself most strongly felt when we come into touch with that form of piety as it really existed, not as we make the best of it for ourselves.'[3] This means two things: first, that the thought of the New Testament should be presented in all the strangeness of historical distance and in the full measure of its antiquity; secondly, that Dr Schweitzer is not indifferent to the relevance of the New Testament for contemporary thought. On the contrary, it is his conviction that the best interests of relevance are served by ignoring it and simply elucidating the thought of the New Testament.

In this methodological attitude Dr Schweitzer has, it seems to me, at the outset an advantage over Professor Dodd. He is delivered from the overwhelming temptation to read his own thoughts into the text lest the New Testament be found to be so antiquated that it no longer speaks to us across the historical void. He is willing to follow wherever the thought seems to lead. This frame of mind has, according to Dr Schweitzer, accounted for the most advance in the study of the life of Jesus. And yet this method too has its dangers. As Dr Schweitzer sees it, 'there is really no other means of arriving at the order and inner con-

---

[1] *Interpreters*, p. vi.   [2] op. cit., p. v.
[3] *Mysticism*, p. ix.

42

nexion of the facts of the life of Jesus (or the thought of Paul) than the making and testing of hypotheses'.[1] But should a hypothesis be followed even when it is seen to lead to absurdities? Dr Schweitzer seems to think so. It is his opinion that, in the history of the study of the life of Jesus, 'it is not the most orderly narratives, those which weave in conscientiously every detail of the text, which have advanced the study of the subject, but precisely the eccentric ones, those that take the greatest liberties with the text'.[2] It remains to be seen whether his exposition of Paul's thought is only a tangential hypothesis which for the sake of methodological consistency takes the greatest liberties with the text of the epistles.

With just one more observation on Dr Schweitzer's method, we shall be prepared to appreciate the meaning and significance of the term 'consistent eschatology'. In *Paul and His Interpreters* Dr Schweitzer's critical comments on previous attempts at understanding Paul reveal his own standards. (The book is in fact an implicit preview of nearly all that appears in *The Mysticism of Paul the Apostle*.) Thus when he comments that the works of eight writers 'do not aim at understanding and showing the development of this doctrine from a single fundamental thought', we perceive that Dr Schweitzer looks for some root idea from which the whole springs. A piecemeal, disconnected description will not satisfy him.

Dr Schweitzer finds this single fundamental thought, this root, idea, to be eschatology, both in the case of Jesus and of Paul. It is for him the key to the life of Jesus, for 'the atmosphere of the time was saturated with eschatology'.[3] 'We must always make a fresh effort to realise to ourselves, that Jesus and his immediate followers were, at that time, in an enthusiastic state of intense eschatological expectation.'[4] 'The teaching of Jesus does not in any of its aspects go outside the Jewish world of thought and project itself into a non-Jewish world, but represents a deeply ethical and perfected version of the contemporary Apocalyptic.'[5] Moreover, what holds for Jesus holds also for Paul, 'for Paul shares with Jesus the eschatological world-view and the eschatological expectation, with all that these imply'.[6] Therefore in *Paul and His Interpreters* Schweitzer predicts the course he will follow in *The Mysticism of Paul the*

[1] *Quest*, p. 7. [2] op. cit., p. 9. [3] *Quest*, p. 348.
[4] op. cit., p. 384. [5] *Interpreters*, p. ix. [5] *Mysticism*, p. 113.

43

Apostle. 'They [the supposed investigators of Pauline thought] will naturally endeavour to find out how far the exclusively eschatological conception of the Gospel manifests its influence in the thoughts of the Apostle of the Gentiles, and will take into account the possibility that his system, strange as this may at first sight appear, may have developed wholly and solely out of that conception.'[1] And, as will be seen later, the eschatological explanations of Jesus and of Paul lead to the solution of the problem of the development of dogma from Jesus to Asia Minor theology. In short, Dr Schweitzer finds the solution to all his Biblical problems by the thorough, consistent application of eschatology as the fundamental framework which alone makes possible a unified comprehension of Christian thought up until Greek theology. For this reason his thought has been termed 'consistent eschatology'.

In real contradiction to Professor Dodd, the kind of eschatology which Dr Schweitzer finds is futuristic, apocalyptic, and world-denying. If the two systems of interpretation were labelled similarly, Dr Schweitzer's would be 'futuristic eschatology' as opposed to 'realised eschatology'. As if to anticipate Professor Dodd's objections, Dr Schweitzer points out that the eschatology of John the Baptist, Jesus, and Paul cannot be simply disposed of as a pitiable attempt to compensate for adverse times. 'The ultimate *differentia* of this eschatology is that it was not, like the other apocalyptic movements, called into existence by historical events. . . . This wave of apocalyptic enthusiasm . . . was called forth . . . solely by the appearance of two great personalities. It is the only time when that ever happened in Jewish eschatology.'[2]

Dr Schweitzer singles Paul out for special attention since he is the link which must be explained to understand the development of dogma from Jesus to the later Greek theology. 'The system of the Apostle of the Gentiles stands over against the teaching of Jesus as something of an entirely different character, and does not create the impression of having arisen out of it. . . . From Paulinism, again, there are no visible lines of connexion leading to early Greek theology.'[3] If Paul can be explained, then perhaps the history of dogma may be put on a firm basis.

---

[1] *Interpreters*, pp. x, xi. [2] *Quest*, p. 368.
[3] *Interpreters*, p. vii.

2. *Paul's system*

The connexion between Jesus and Paul sets us off to a 'consistent eschatology' analysis of Paul's thought since Dr Schweitzer sees that they share the same eschatological world-view. In commenting on Baur he reveals his own sentiments. 'Baur admits that the Apostle fully shared the faith of the primitive community in the nearness of the *parousia*, and was at one with it in all the conceptions referring to the End.'[1] Again Lipsius anticipates Dr Schweitzer when 'he assumes that the thought of the *parousia* gives an inner unity to the Apostle's ideas'. This is the foreshadowing of the application of the 'consistent eschatology' principle which seeks to explain all by means of eschatology. The same suggestion appears in Dr Schweitzer's satisfaction with Titius that 'in the examination of the individual views' he 'always takes the future hope as his starting-point. . .'.[2] Kabisch has shown that 'eschatology is the foundation of the dogmatics and ethics of the Apostle'.[3]

What does 'eschatology' mean? 'The term eschatology ought only to be applied when reference is made to the end of the world as expected in the immediate future, and the events, hopes, and fears connected therewith.'[4] This kind of eschatology was precisely that which is found in Paul. Even in his later writings Paul holds on to his belief in a speedy return of Christ, for 'it is . . . not the fact that Paul in the Epistle to the Philippians is less confident about the speedy Return of Jesus than he was earlier'.[5] He expressly rejects the idea that Paul, as Professor Dodd attempts to show, changed his ideas about eschatology. 'The conception of the things of the End is a unity, and remains the same throughout.'[6] 'From his first letter to his last Paul's thought is uniformly dominated by the expectation of the immediate return of Jesus, of the Judgment, and the Messianic glory.'[7] Paul's conception of the End is apocalyptic. The word Dr Schweitzer uses to describe it is '*naturhaft*', translated 'physical'. It means that what is to take place at the End 'is not a question of a purely spiritual redemption, but that the whole physical and hyperphysical being of the man is thereby translated into a new condition. Body and soul are redeemed together; and in such a way that not only the elect portion

[1] op. cit., p. 21. [2] *Interpreters*, p. 157. [3] op. cit., p. 58.
[4] op. cit., p. 228. [5] *Mysticism*, p. 135.
[6] *Interpreters*, p. 74. [7] *Mysticism*, p. 52.

45

of mankind, but the whole world is completely transformed in a great catastrophic event.'[1]

This eschatology determines Paul's idea of redemption. 'In its primary and fundamental sense' redemption 'consists in a deliverance from the powers which have their abode between heaven and earth. It is therefore essentially a future good, dependent on a cosmic event of universal scope.'[2] But this does not mean that redemption was completely future in the sense in which it was before Jesus' death and resurrection. 'The conception of Redemption which stands behind this eschatological expectation is, to put it quite generally, that Jesus Christ has made an end of the natural world and is bringing in the Messianic Kingdom.'[3] 'Everywhere is apparent the tendency of the Pauline teaching to represent the Coming Redemption as having already begun to come into operation.'[4] 'In the death of Jesus begins the cessation of the natural world, and in His resurrection the dawning of the supernatural world.'[5]

The attempt to express this already-fulfilled aspect of eschatological redemption leads Dr Schweitzer to what he feels to be the centre of Paul's thought, i.e. the mysticism of being-in-Christ. But the newness of Dr Schweitzer's insight is that this mysticism is only intelligible in terms of eschatology. This is evident from the fact that Paul's is a Christ-mysticism without being a God-mysticism. 'The peculiarity that the mysticism of Paul is only a mysticism of being-in-Christ, and not also a mysticism of being-in-God, has thus its foundation in the fact that it originally had its place in an eschatological world-view.'[6] In fact the hallmark of Paul's mysticism is its eschatology. 'The fact that it occurs in connexion with the expectation of the end of the world, and is founded upon cosmic events, gives its distinctive character to the Pauline mysticism.'[7]

Paul's use of Hellenistic terms to express this mysticism led commentators off on the wrong track of attempting to derive Paul's thought from Greek non-eschatological sources. But when once the eschatological impulse behind Paul's thought is appreciated, 'then Paulinism is understood, since in its essence it can be nothing else than an eschatological mysticism, expressing itself by the aid of the Greek religious terminology.'[8]

[1] *Interpreters*, p. 162, n. 3. [2] op. cit., p. 57. [3] *Mysticism*, p. 54.
[4] op. cit., p. 64. [5] *Mysticism*, p. 23. [6] *Mysticism*, p. 13.
[7] op. cit., p. 23. [8] *Interpreters*, p. 241.

46

The content of the Greek terms was completely determined by the Jewish eschatological thought of Paul.

Being basically eschatological, this being-in-Christ mysticism expresses itself in terms of death and resurrection in mystical participation with Christ. Because His resurrection ushered in the future, by sharing that death and resurrection, the believer may also share in the future blessings in a preliminary way. 'The fact to which for him [Paul] mysticism . . . [goes] back is the dying and rising again of Christ, which took place in the immediate past. This fact is a cosmic event. In the death of Jesus begins the cessation of the natural world, and in His resurrection the dawning of the supernatural world. This cosmic event translates itself in the created being, man, as a dying and rising again.'[1]

For Dr Schweitzer, however, the prime importance of this dying and rising again is to put the believer in a position of advantage over other men. This dying and rising with Christ marks out those who are to participate in the first resurrection to the Messianic kingdom. 'Paul's conception is, that believers in mysterious fashion share the dying and rising again of Christ, and in this way are swept away out of their ordinary mode of existence, and form a special category of humanity. When the Messianic Kingdom dawns, those of them who are still in life are not natural men like others, but men who have in some way passed through death and resurrection along with Christ, and are thus capable of becoming partakers of the resurrection mode of existence, while other men pass under dominion of death.'[2] It seems to me that here we come upon the weakest part of Dr Schweitzer's exposition of Paul, namely in the claim that the Apostle held to two Resurrections, a Messianic and a General, and to two corresponding blessednesses, a temporary and an eternal. Paul is supposed to be the creator of this doctrine of the two Resurrections.[3] In support of this Dr Schweitzer cites 1 Cor. 15.50-3 but has to admit at once that 'so far as the wording goes, Paul might have been speaking of the resurrection of the dead in general'.[4] Then how do we know that two resurrections are intended behind the wording? Dr

[1] *Mysticism*, p. 23.   [2] *Mysticism*, p. 23.   [3] op. cit., p. 94.
[4] ibid. Professor J. Héring makes the same observation. 'Schweitzer recognises that the second resurrection is not even mentioned in 1 Cor. 15 and we maintain that we have not found it anywhere else.' J. Héring, 'Saint Paul a-t-il enseigné deux résurrections?' p. 304.

Schweitzer says, by consulting 1 Thess. 4.16 and 1 Cor. 15.23. But neither of these mention two resurrections. Then where did Dr Schweitzer get the idea? We have to do here with an over-enthusiasm for the role which eschatological problems played in the development of Paul's thought. It is an exaggeration to say that 'the first and most immediate problem' of the Christian faith 'was the temporal separation of the Resurrection and Return of Jesus Christ', and that Paul's whole system of thought is an endeavour to answer this single problem.[1]

Now some have fastened on to this problem of the delay of the Parousia as indicated by Dr Schweitzer, have treated it as though this delay endangered the faith of the early Church, and have drawn the conclusion that the embarrassment of this error about the Parousia proves that the whole structure of the New Testament is shaky and that the only course is to conclude 'that faith must be independent of history'.[2] But as Professor Cullmann has pointed out, the delay of the Parousia did not diminish hope or endanger faith. The true question which it called forth was: 'How did it happen that the hope in the sphere of the New Testament remained unshaken in spite of the fact that a delay of the Parousia was realised from the start?'[3] And the answer to this question is that New Testament faith was not shaken because of 'the effects ascribed to the Holy Spirit and experienced in the time of the authors'.[4] Although Dr Schweitzer may have misread the problem, nevertheless the answer was not overlooked, for he sees that in Paul the Spirit is the bearer of future blessedness in the present.

3. The Spirit

Dr Schweitzer entitles *Mysticism*, Ch. VIII, 'Possession of the Spirit as a Mode of Manifestation of the Being-risen-with-Christ'. His treatment of the Spirit in this chapter is the climax of the treatment of the temporal tension between fulfilment and consummation to which Dr Schweitzer has often alluded. 'A resurrection of the dead was only to take place when the supernatural age had dawned. If Jesus has risen, that means, for those who dare to think consistently, that it is now already

[1] *Mysticism*, p. 111.
[2] Buri, 'Zur Diskussion des Problems der ausgebliebenen Parusie', p. 426.
[3] Cullmann, 'Das wahre durch die ausgebliebene Parusie gestellte neutestamentliche Problem', p. 178.
[4] Cullmann, op. cit., p. 179.

48

the supernatural age. And this is Paul's point of view. He cannot regard the resurrection of Jesus as an isolated event, but must regard it as the initial event of the rising of the dead in general.'[1] Consequently the future is breaking into the present, as one of Dr Schweitzer's favourite verses (1 Cor. 10.11) suggests is possible. 'Through the Resurrection of Jesus it had become manifest that resurrection powers, that is to say, powers of the supernatural world, were already at work within the created world. Those who had insight, therefore, did not reckon the duration of the natural world as up to the coming of Jesus in glory, but conceived of the intervening time between His Resurrection and the beginning of the Messianic Kingdom as a time when the natural and the supernatural world are inter-mingled.'[2] And the resurrection powers referred to are the Spirit.

Without ever calling attention to the relevant passages to show that the Spirit was the power that raised up Jesus and thus made His resurrection one of the first-fruits of His action, Dr Schweitzer gives a prominent place to the Christocentric nature of the Spirit. In fact, in one place Dr Schweitzer goes farther than Paul, who says that the Spirit is given by the Father only by stating that 'the Holy Spirit, therefore, comes to the believer from Christ. . .'.[3] But by and large the relation of the Spirit to Christ is well brought out. 'It is the life-principle of His Messianic personality and of the state of existence characteristic of the Messianic Kingdom.'[4] 'If God's Spirit is poured out after the resurrection of Christ, that means that it is poured out in consequence of that resurrection.'[5]

The Spirit is related to the future as well. 'In regarding the possession of the Spirit as a sign of the resurrection which is already in process of being realised in the believer', Paul is going beyond his theological forerunners.[6] 'Paul was the first to arrive at the conception of risen men who are also vehicles of the Spirit.'[7] 'The Spirit is the earnest, given to be a possession of their hearts, of the coming glory.'[8] 'The possession of the Spirit proves to believers that they are already removed out of the natural state of existence and transferred into the supernatural.'[9] Some of the concrete benefits of the Spirit's presence

[1] *Mysticism*, p. 98.   [2] op. cit., pp. 98-9.   [3] *Mysticism*, p. 165.
[4] ibid.   [5] ibid.   [6] op. cit., p. 160.
[7] op. cit., p. 164.   [8] op. cit., p. 166.   [9] op. cit., p. 167.

are: the true circumcision of the heart; the New Covenant; the New Law which gives life; assurance of adoption and justification and that the believer is loved by God. Much of what is said in this excellent chapter is repetition of statements scattered through *Interpreters*, of which at least one is worth quoting and amounts to a comment on 1 Cor. 15.45: 'He [Christ] is the "life-giving spirit" because the *pneuma* which goes forth from Him as the glorified Christ works in believers as the power of the resurrection.'[1]

Conclusion

But the difficulty of all this excellent statement of doctrine is that it stands under the cloud of Dr Schweitzer's doctrine of two resurrections, *plus* a certain fuzziness of Christology. And the combination of his eschatology and his Christology enables Dr Schweitzer eventually to separate the Spirit from Christ, for the Messiah and His blessedness were both time-conditioned conceptions which have no claim to continuing validity beyond the period of primitive Christianity. When Dr Schweitzer suggests the programme of creative theology necessary for today, it amounts to the recommendation of a shift from the eschatological-Christological Spirit of Paul to a reliance on 'the Spirit' pure and simple. 'An explanation which shows that the Apostle's system is based on the most primitive eschatological premises . . . at the same time makes it intelligible why subsequent generations could not continue to follow the road on which he started.'[2] Paul's doctrine is of no immediate use since 'it may no doubt prove to be the case that this "positive" criticism will appear distressingly negative to those who look for results which can be immediately coined into dogmatic and homiletic currency'.[3] And what is the alternative without the direction of Paul's doctrine? The answer is to become 'followers of Paul, believing in the Spirit', and thus on the basis of this belief in the Spirit be enabled to 'walk secure and undismayed'.[4] *Mysticism* ends with the same suggestion to leave Paul behind and follow the Spirit. 'Since the world conditions have changed, we can do no other than think our own thoughts about the redemptive significance of the death of Jesus and all that is connected with it, basing our thoughts, *so far as possible*[5] on the original and

---

[1] *Interpreters*, p. 221.   [2] op. cit., p. 249.   [3] op. cit., p. 249.
[4] ibid.   [5] Italics mine.

Primitive-Christian doctrine. . . . Instead of simply being able to take over traditional material as we find it, we must, exactly as did Ignatius and Justin, recast it by a creative act of the Spirit.'[1]

However, the overdrawn eschatology of the Messianic blessedness to which Dr Schweitzer confines Paul's doctrine of Christ and the Spirit overlooks the unavoidably permanent element in Paul's doctrine of the Spirit. This permanent element is his *kyrios* Christology, with which the Spirit is intimately bound.[2] 'The Pauline Christ, however, even though He is called the Son of God, is not God, but only a heavenly Being.'[3] 'It is also to be remarked that, on the other hand, there is no "Redeemer-god" in Primitive Christianity. Jesus is, it cannot be sufficiently emphasised, not thought of as a god, but only as a heavenly being, who is entrusted with the mission of bringing in the new world. . . . For Paul he is "Son of God" in the simple Old Testament . . . sense.'[4] Unfortunately Dr Schweitzer overlooks the fact that in that same simple Old Testament sense He is for Paul 'the Lord', and that makes Him precisely God. That the Spirit is for Paul the Spirit of Jesus, of Christ, and is the Lord, shows that his doctrine of the Spirit is bound up with all aspects of his Christology.

In the last analysis, Paul's eschatology and pneumatology are determined by his Christology, and Dr Schweitzer's error lies in trying to reverse the process. For Paul, Christ reigned as Lord at the Father's right hand, and would continue to do so until the consummation. If Paul was correct here then the same situation must continue to hold for us. And because the Spirit is the Lord, it is difficult to see how Paul's doctrine of the Spirit could be valid for him and not for us also. But Dr Schweitzer overlooked the permanent normative element in Pauline Christology and thus was able to consign Paul's thought to obsolescence. But if Dr Schweitzer were consistent, then the Spirit must be consigned to antiquity also, for Pauline Christology and pneumatology are inseparable. That Dr Schweitzer should have held on to the Spirit as the timeless element in Primitive Christianity shows that his doctrine of the Spirit goes back to nineteenth-century presuppositions rather than Paul. As Professor Wilder has observed, Schweitzer's work rested on

---

[1] *Mysticism*, p. 291. [2] See above, Ch. I. on 2 Cor. 3.18.
[3] *Interpreters*, p. 223. [4] op. cit., p. 194.

'rationalist and Hegelian assumptions' similar to those of Harnack, and he 'took refuge in an ethical mysticism which has its links with the timeless values of his predecessors . . .'.[1]

Holmstroem also traces Dr Schweitzer's real presupposition to the nineteenth century. He characterises the position of *Mysticism* as a 'timeless, ethical, volitional mysticism,' and remarks that 'Schweitzer now has come, still more than Ritschl, to a one-sided, inner-worldly and ethical conception of the innermost essence of the Christian religion'.[2]

Dr Schweitzer's only logical choice was to accept the Spirit as an integral part of Paul's thought or else reject Paul and the Spirit with him. That he kept the Spirit but discarded Paul shows that he did not perceive the interdependence of the Spirit and the Lord which we attempted to show in Ch. I.

But no matter how subsequent scholarship may find it necessary to correct the results of the application of Dr Schweitzer's hypothesis to Paul, it will always be in his debt for calling attention to the eschatological aspect of all of his thought, and particularly to the eschatological aspect of his doctrine of the Spirit.

[1] Wilder, *Eschatology and Ethics in the Teaching of Jesus*, p. 45.
[2] Holmstroem, *Das eschatologische Denken der Gegenwart*, p. 99.

V

C. H. DODD'S REALISED ESCHATOLOGY

1. 'Realised eschatology'

PROFESSOR DODD'S eschatological point of view is summed up in the phrase which he himself uses to designate it—'realised eschatology'.[1] The phrase occurs first in the writings of 1935, although the previous works show a tendency toward the same eschatology. In dealing with the meaning of Jesus' ministry it is used to sum up the basic presupposition. After an argument to prove that the Kingdom of God has come, Professor Dodd draws the implications. 'This declaration that the Kingdom of God has already come necessarily dislocates the whole eschatological scheme in which its expected coming closes the long vista of the future. The *eschaton* has moved from the future to the present, from the sphere of expectation into that of realised experience.'[2] 'Here then is the fixed point from which our interpretation of the teaching regarding the Kingdom of God must start. It represents the ministry of Jesus as "realised eschatology", that is to say, as the impact upon this world of the "powers of the world to come" in a series of events, unprecedented and unrepeatable, now in actual process.'[3] In Jesus' ministry 'God is confronting [men] in His kingdom, power, and glory. This world has become the scene of a divine drama. It is the hour of decision. It is realised eschatology.'[4]

[1] In this chapter six works of Professor Dodd will be used. In order to simplify the footnoting, the following abbreviations will represent their corresponding titles. The arrangement is chronological.
(a) Romans = The Epistle of Paul to the Romans, London 1932.
(b) Studies = New Testament Studies, Manchester 1953. (The two papers under consideration are 'The Mind of Paul: I', 1933, and 'The Mind of Paul: II', 1934.)
(c) Parables = The Parables of the Kingdom, London 1935. (Based on a course of lectures delivered in the spring of 1935.)
(d) Preaching = The Apostolic Preaching and Its Developments, with an appendix on Eschatology and History, London 1936. (A course of lectures delivered in 1935.)
(e) History = History and the Gospel, London 1938.
(f) Scriptures = According to the Scriptures, the Substructure of New Testament Theology, London 1952. (A revision of a course of lectures delivered in March 1950.)
[2] Parables, p. 50.   [3] op. cit., p. 51.   [4] op. cit., p. 198.

To Paul belongs the credit for the first theology of this eschatology. 'It is in the epistles of Paul . . . that full justice is done for the first time to the principle of "realised eschatology" which is vital to the whole *kerygma*. That supernatural order of life which the apocalyptists had predicted in terms of pure fantasy is now described as an actual fact of experience.'[1] John carries out the same principle with more thorough-going consistency, 'deliberately subordinating the "futurist" eschatology of the early Church to the "realised eschatology" '.[2] In fact, after citing passages from Matthew, Acts, Paul, Hebrews, 1 Peter, and John, Professor Dodd feels justified in concluding that 'for the New Testament writers in general, the *eschaton* has entered history; . . . the Age to come has come. The Gospel of primitive Christianity is a Gospel of realised eschatology.'[3]

It seems clear then what Professor Dodd intends to express by his term 'realised eschatology'. All the future elements in eschatology, the hoped-for last things, the consummation of redemption, the future Age—these have all been present since the Advent of Jesus Christ. This is not just Professor Dodd's view of eschatology, nor that of only a segment of New Testament thought. He claims it as the view of New Testament Christianity.

2. *Professor Dodd's concern*

Behind every particular theological point of view lies a particular concern which that theology expresses or implements. Professor Dodd does not explicitly say that this is the case with him. It is perhaps to his credit that he does not, since that might lead to a theology which has become a means to an end rather than an exposition of the thought of the New Testament. In spite of this silence on the part of Professor Dodd, it does seem wise for the sake of an attempt at a sympathetic understanding of his point of view that we look for his concern. At the risk of misinterpreting 'realised eschatology', I suggest that the primary concern it expresses is to make the Gospel relevant to modern history and the life of today without at all sacrificing anything of the truth of the Gospel. This concern becomes especially evident in a treatment of the relation between history and the Gospel, for in this relation both the offence

[1] *Preaching*, p. 65. The same argument is summed up in *History*, p. 30.
[2] *Preaching*, p. 66.   [3] op. cit., p. 85.

which belongs to the Gospel and its relevance become evident.

Professor Dodd's exposition of the apostolic preaching ends by raising the problem of relevance with the question, 'How far can it be preached in the twentieth century?' At the same time he rejects that mistaken attempt of theology which 'tried to believe that criticism could prune away from the New Testament those elements in it which seemed to us fantastic, and leave us with an original "essence of Christianity", to which modern man could say, "This is what I have always thought".'[1] He considers rather a study of the primitive Christian preaching, confronting it in the strange terms of its day, to be the first step toward genuine relevance. 'The Gospel itself can never be other than it was at the beginning.'[2] How then is this originality and relevance expressed in terms of the Gospel and history?

The offence of the Gospel which must be retained is its particularity. In terms of history this expresses the Gospel's uniqueness. 'For Christianity . . . the eternal God is revealed in history.'[3] This revelation does not take place in history generally, nor is it a matter of indifference which events are chosen as revelation. The coming of Jesus Christ, His ministry, death and resurrection, were the unique and absolute self-revelation of God.[4] Christianity is committed to 'the scandal of particularity' (quoting Professor Gerhard Kittel in *Mysterium Christi*), which means 'a view which selects one particular episode in history, and declares that it possesses an absolute and final quality distinguishing it from all other events'.[5]

The relevance of the Gospel is its eschatology. 'The New Testament writers are clear that history is henceforward qualitatively different from what it was before Christ's coming. . . . The "Christian Era", as we call it, marks an abrupt break in the relation in which the people of God, and indeed, the whole human race, stands to the historical order.'[6] Precisely because this eschatology is a realised eschatology which concentrates on the present and withholds nothing for the future, nor insists on hope in what is not yet seen, it is relevant. The traditional conception of eschatology with its outstanding, not yet realised, promised benefits raises rather than solves the problem of relevance. In the light of its irrelevance, it is not surprising to find

---

[1] *Preaching*, p. 76.   [2] *History*, p. 163.   [3] op. cit., p. 23.
[4] This point is developed in *Preaching*, beginning with p. 87.
[5] *Preaching*, p. 88.   [6] ibid.

that Professor Dodd betrays a certain antipathy toward the futuristic and apocalyptic elements in traditional eschatology.

3. *Antipathy to apocalyptic*

This antipathy is evident in an attempt to account for the apocalyptic frame of mind psychologically. 'Now Jewish apocalyptic has some very noble elements, but from a psychological point of view it must be described as a form of compensation in fantasy for the sense of futility and defeat. Historically it was bred of the despair of the world which fell on the Jews under acute and prolonged oppression. . . . There is no acceptance of life as it is, or reconciliation to experience as it comes, for we do not meet God in it. We set ourselves against the actual world, believing that God is with us, but not in it. We expect of Him that He will vindicate us at the expense of all else. This apocalyptic represents the apotheosis of a personal claim upon reality for satisfaction, power, and vindication.'[1] This leads to the first objection to apocalyptic. It denies the present world order. Apocalyptic involves 'a certain harsh dualism—the dualism of "things of the Lord" and "things of the world", of "this age" and "the age to come", of the "elect" and the rest of humanity, of redeemed humanity and the whole living universe.'[2] Apocalyptic eschatology . . . implies a radical devaluation of the present world order in all its aspects.'[3] At this point Jesus departed from His heritage. 'This sense of the divineness of the natural order is the major premise of all the parables, and it is the point where Jesus differs most profoundly from the outlook of the Jewish apocalyptists. . . .'[4] By contrast to apocalyptic otherworldliness Professor Dodd prefers 'a recognition of natural human goodness, of the relative value of human institutions, and of the possibility of taking them up into the Christian life'.[5]

The second objection to apocalyptic is its futurism. 'An exclusive concentration of attention upon glory to come, with the corresponding devaluation of the present, its duties and opportunities, its social claims and satisfactions, obscures the finer and more humane aspects of morality.'[6] To this Professor Dodd prefers a subordinating of the 'futurist' element in the eschatology of the early Church to 'realised eschatology'.[7]

[1] *Studies*, 'The Mind of Paul: II', pp. 126-7.   [2] op. cit., p. 126.
[3] op. cit., p. 113.   [4] *Parables*, p. 22.
[5] *Studies*, 'The Mind of Paul: II', p. 118.
[6] *Preaching*, p. 64.   [7] op. cit., p. 66.

Finally, apocalyptic is objectionable because it has no relevance to the present. 'It works with the prophetic scheme of history, but with certain differences. In particular, it virtually gives up the attempt to recognise divine meaning in the present. The mighty hand of the Lord is to be seen in events of the remote past, and will again be seen in the future, but in the present the power of evil obscures it.'[1]

Of course anyone who chooses to take this attitude toward apocalyptic and futuristic thinking must recognise the difficulty of interpreting the thought of the New Testament, for this apocalyptic element is present in all of its strata. Professor Dodd recognises this difficulty of New Testament strains of thought inconsistent with 'realised eschatology'. For example the Revelation of John 'falls below the ethical ideals of the prophets'.[2] In addition to the obvious case of Revelation, apocalyptic elements are admitted in the form of Jesus' teaching in the Synoptics, in Mark 13, in Thessalonians, in 1 Peter, and in 1 John. How then are these elements to be explained so that 'realised eschatology' remains the true reading of New Testament thought? Professor Dodd disposes of apocalyptic elements in the New Testament in three ways.

In the first place apocalyptic elements are disposed of by attributing them to Jewish influences in Christian thinking which have not yet been replaced by the Gospel. By this statement I do not mean to imply that Professor Dodd belittles the Hebrew heritage of the Christian religion. Nothing could be farther from the truth. His work *According to the Scriptures* is solely devoted to an appreciation of the Old Testament background of New Testament theology. The Old Testament's contribution to the New is outstandingly a positive and creative one. For Professor Dodd it is more important than the Hellenistic contribution. But this one element of apocalyptic is an aberration. It reaches its climax within the New Testament in the *Revelation of John*. 'As a piece of apocalyptic literature it takes its place naturally in the series which begins with the Book of Daniel, and includes such works as the Book of Enoch, the Assumption of Moses, the Apocalypse of Baruch, and 2 Esdras. . . . The whole emphasis falls on that which is to come. The other elements in the *kerygma* are indeed present as a background . . . [but the] excessive emphasis on the future has the effect

[1] op. cit., p. 80. [2] *Preaching*, p. 64.

E

57

of relegating to a secondary place just those elements in the original Gospel which are most distinctive of Christianity. . . . Under the danger of this revived Jewish eschatology, Christianity was in danger of falling back into the position of the earlier apocalyptists. . . . In the second century its stream of thought ran out into the barren sands of millennarianism, which in the end was disavowed by the Church.'[1] Not only does Revelation fall below Christian standards eschatologically but also in regard to its doctrine of God. 'The God of the Apocalypse can hardly be recognised as the Father of our Lord Jesus Christ, nor has the fierce Messiah, whose warriors ride in blood up to their horses' bridles, many traits that could recall Him of whom the primitive *kerygma* proclaimed that He went about doing good and healing all who were oppressed by the devil, because God was with Him.'[2] To Professor Dodd it is obvious that Revelation does not belong to the record of Christian revelation. The 'Little Apocalypse' of Mark 13 has suffered from the same influence, and 'though it contains embedded in it sayings belonging to the primitive tradition of the teaching of Jesus, it is inconsistent with the purport of His teaching as a whole. . . .'[3] This same unhealthy Jewish influence is evident to Professor Dodd in 2 Thess. 1.7-10.

Secondly, apocalyptic elements are disposed of by reinterpreting eschatology in terms of the absolute or supernatural rather than the temporal, by replacing teleology with purpose. Although Professor Dodd does not expressly make this point, it is clearly his meaning. 'Eschatology is not itself the substance of the Gospel, but a form under which the absolute value of the Gospel facts is asserted.'[4] In describing redemption 'ultimate' and 'eschatological' are used synonymously.[5] 'All these are "eschatological" in character; they are ultimates, and are proper not to this empirical realm of time and space, but to the absolute order.'[6] With this non-temporal eschatology it becomes possible to escape time altogether. Referring to those passages in the Gospels which predict a second advent of the Son of Man it can now be said that 'these future tenses are only an accommodation of language. There is no coming of the Son of Man "after" His coming in Galilee and Jerusalem, whether soon or late, for there is no before and after in the

---

[1] op. cit., pp. 39-41. [2] op. cit., p. 41. [3] op. cit., p. 38.
[4] op. cit., p. 42. [5] op. cit., p. 43. [6] *Parables*, p. 107.

eternal order.'[1] Eschatology expresses itself in history, for Professor Dodd, not as a teleology with a real goal at a future point in time but as the continual working out of God's purpose. 'In Christianity the teleological "end" is other than the temporal end of the process', by which is meant that the event of Christ's first coming, ministry, death and resurrection give meaning and purpose to all history without any future goal being necessary.[2] Professor Dodd states repeatedly, however, that he does not deny the reality of time. Nevertheless the Cross is the 'end', not the centre, of history. This replacing of teleology with purpose is best expressed in Professor Dodd's summary of the meaning of history. 'History, therefore, as a process of redemption and revelation, has a beginning and an end, both in God. The beginning is not an event in time; the end is not an event in time. The beginning is God's purpose, the end is the fulfilment of His purpose.'[3]

Thirdly, Professor Dodd disposes of apocalyptic elements in the New Testament by importing a Platonic conception of the relation of God to history and a Platonic conception of time. These conceptions of God and the Kingdom as absolutes and of time as endless were already implicit in Professor Dodd's reinterpretation of the traditional idea of eschatology. As with Plato, history is for Professor Dodd the incomplete and imperfect striving of this world of time and space after the transcendent Absolutes of eternity. In Christian terms, this Absolute becomes the Kingdom which entered history, and continues to challenge and guide history, but without ever becoming a part of history. Because of this absolute nature of the Kingdom, Jesus 'could not ally Himself with any of the historical movements of His time', since He was 'the bearer of a Kingdom which is altogether other than the relativities of human existence'.[4] In Professor Dodd's view, Paul, John, and the author of Hebrews all make use of a Platonic system of thought to do away with Jewish apocalyptic. 'In [John's] Gospel even more fully than in Paul, eschatology is sublimated into a distinctive kind of mysticism. Its underlying philosophy, like that of the Epistle to the Hebrews, is of a Platonic cast. . . . The ultimate reality, instead of being, as in Jewish apocalyptic, figured as the last term in the historical series, is conceived as an eternal order

---

[1] op. cit., p. 108. [2] *History*, p. 165.
[3] op. cit., p. 171. [4] op. cit., p. 128.

59

of being, of which the phenomenal order in history is the shadow or symbol. This eternal order is the Kingdom of God, into which Christians have been born again, by water and the Spirit (3.3-8). . . . This is the Johannine equivalent for . . . the Pauline declaration that if any man is in Christ there is a new creation.'[1] 'In the Epistle to the Hebrews eschatology has been reinterpreted in terms of a Platonic scheme. The "Age to Come" is identified with that order of eternal reality whose shadows or reflections form the world of phenomena.'[2] Professor Dodd is obviously pleased with this Platonic scheme as the vehicle of New Testament thought, and he carries the same scheme into his understanding of time.

A beginning and an end to time are for Professor Dodd inconceivable. 'Creation and Last Judgment are symbolic statements of the truth that all history is teleological, working out one universal divine purpose.'[3] And 'that the succession of events in time will one day cease . . . is . . . an idea as inconceivable to us as its opposite.'[4] His idea of time comes most sharply to the fore in the following two sentences. 'For it is in the nature of our time experience that it cannot be bounded either before or after. It is, indeed, in this sense that time is, as Plato said, the "moving image of eternity".'[5] The express relation of Platonism to New Testament theology is no occasion for alarm to Professor Dodd. Although the conclusion of his *According to the Scriptures* is that the fundamental substructure of the theology of the New Testament is Biblical, i.e. Hebraic, he feels, nevertheless, that 'it is certainly true that the development of Christian theology was profoundly influenced by the religious thought of Hellenism, and it cannot be questioned that this influence is already at work in the New Testament, notably in some parts of the Pauline epistles, in the Epistle to the Hebrews, and in the Fourth Gospel'. Professor Dodd is not, he goes on, 'among those who deplore' the influence of those theologians who used Greek philosophy, nor is he persuaded by those who tell us that the great task of theologians of this generation is to purge Christian theology of the last dregs of Platonism.[6]

So far, the purpose of this chapter has been to give, unencumbered by criticism and illustrating each point with Professor

---

[1] *Preaching*, pp. 66-7.   [2] op. cit., p. 45.   [3] *History*, p. 168.
[4] op. cit., p. 170.   [5] *Preaching*, pp. 87-8.   [6] *Scriptures*, p. 139.

Dodd's own words, an accurate exposition of the salient features of 'realised eschatology'. All this has been merely preparatory to a critical examination of his treatment of Paul's eschatology and doctrine of the Spirit.

4. *'Realised eschatology' and Paul*

Professor Dodd's exposition of Pauline thought is an attempt to show that, although the apostle began his theological thinking with a strongly apocalyptic, Jewish eschatology, his letters show a development away from these beginnings to a realised eschatology. At the outset it must be observed by the way of criticism that there is a strong presumption against any considerable change in Paul's thought—and the change that Professor Dodd suggests is considerable. At the time of the authorship of the first epistle (1 Thessalonians) which gives us evidence of Paul's theology, the Apostle, according to Professor Dodd's own chronology 'was at least forty years old, probably older. He had been a Christian for fifteen years or more, a trained theologian before that, and an active Christian teacher for at least twelve years, probably longer.' At such an age and with such a background it is highly improbable that Paul's thought would change considerably. Professor Dodd recognises this difficulty but pleads at least for the possibility of a change and the chance to present his case. This should of course be granted, but there is still another presumption against Professor Dodd which he does not mention. As an Apostle, Paul was the bearer of a unique office, and with that office went the strong consciousness evident in Paul's epistles that what he taught was not the result of his own insight but the God-given revelation of what must otherwise remain a mystery. He was conscious of having the mind of Christ. Any considerable change in his theology would have meant the abrogation of the authority of his office. His opponents would certainly have noticed such a change and used it against him. We have no evidence of any such charge in his defences of his Apostleship. It is a mistake to treat Paul as though he were in the same position as a present-day theologian with apostolic gifts who changes his mind as often as his own insights lead him to.

How then does Professor Dodd attempt to discharge his burden of proof? In the first place he attempts to show a psychological change in Paul, a second conversion, which would dispose us to be more kindly toward his contention that Paul had a change of mind to match this change of heart. Professor Dodd's essay 'The Mind of Paul: I'[1] is devoted to this demonstration. The supposed change in Paul took place somewhere between the two letters which constitute 2 Corinthians. The Apostle's conversion had been determinative for his life, but according to Professor Dodd 'we find indications that old ways of thought and traits of character in part survived the change, and were only gradually brought captive to the allegiance of Christ. There is a touchiness about his dignity which sorts ill with the selflessness of one who has died with Christ. When opposition presents itself, he will override it with a rod (1 Cor. 4.21)! When external conditions thwart him, he resents it (1 Thess. 2.18). When illness or nervous exhaustion reduces his efficiency he chafes and frets (2 Cor. 12.7). Unconsciously, perhaps he still yields to the desire to excel. . . .'[2] The letter represented by 2 Cor. 10-13 exhibits this temperament, being written, as Professor Dodd interprets it, 'in a passion of resentment' and 'full of caustic sarcasm and indignant self-vindication'.[3] But the second letter, 2 Cor. 1-9, shows a change of heart. In 2 Cor. 9 he admits to speaking as a fool, and 'the same letter shows how in the depth of his humiliation he found firm ground. "I am strong just when I am weak." . . . There is nothing in earlier letters like the quiet self-abandonment of 2 Cor. 4-5.'[4] And yet it must be observed that in later letters there appears again the self-assertion which Professor Dodd associates with the period before the supposed change between the two letters of 2 Corinthians. It seems that the supposed change did not take place.[5] First let us look at Galatians. Professor Dodd feels that it is probably later than 1 Corinthians.[6] And if later than 1 Corinthians it could well be later than 2 Corinthians. And since Paul's defence of his Apostleship in Gal. 1 and 2 exhibits the attitudes and outlook which Professor Dodd supposes the Apostle to have lost, then the supposed change did not take place. Romans is definitely later than 2 Corinthians and it shows in 1.1-6 and especially 1.11 that Paul still considers himself an authority in spiritual matters because of his unique position as an apostle.

---

[1] *Studies*, p. 83. [2] op. cit., p. 79. [3] op. cit., p. 80. [4] op. cit., pp. 80-1.
[5] There are of course strong arguments for the unity of 2 Corinthians, but so far as possible I prefer to discuss Professor Dodd's theory about Paul's development on the basis of his own presuppositions.
[6] *Studies*, p. 106 n.

In fact, all the differences in tone to be found in Paul's writings are best accounted for in the light of his Apostleship. Whenever and wherever Paul's teaching and authority in the Church was challenged, it was necessary for him to maintain his teaching and assert his authority, but not, as Professor Dodd construes, for personal reasons. The office of Apostle had been thrust upon Paul. He had not asked for it. But now that he had it, his allegiance to his Lord forced him to fulfil it against every challenge. To have acted otherwise would have meant that special revelation would have been replaced by consensus of opinion, with the probable result that Christianity would never have grown beyond the limits of an essentially Jewish sect. The appearance of a change of tone and mood which lends credence to Professor Dodd's theory is simply the result of the fact that all the later letters which we have show Paul in situations in which his teaching and authority were not sharply challenged. If the challenge had come, his apostolic consciousness would have forced him to a defence. Professor Dodd mistakes an apostolic consciousness for peevishness. But Professor Dodd's case does not depend solely on evidence which can be mustered for a psychological spiritual change in Paul. That was only preliminary to the real question. Was there a change in Paul's theology amounting to a shift from primitive Christian apocalyptic eschatology to realised eschatology? We turn to a critical review of Professor Dodd's affirmative answer to the question.

It is clear to Professor Dodd that in Paul's early preaching and in his earlier epistles the futuristic, apocalyptic elements of primitive Christianity were present. His language in Gal. 1.4 'implies the Jewish doctrine of the two ages'.[1] This idea of two ages provided the setting for his understanding of the significance of the facts of Christ's death and resurrection.[2] 'It seems clear that Paul started with eschatological beliefs of the type best represented by such Jewish writings as the Book of Enoch, the Apocalypse of Baruch and the Apocalypse of Ezra.'[3] This included the idea of a future judgment. 'Judgment is for Paul a function of the universal lordship of Christ . . . and His second advent as Judge is part of the *kerygma*.'[4] Along with the second Advent Paul expected the consummation of the new age. 'His

[1] *Preaching*, p. 11.   [2] op. cit., p. 13.
[3] *Studies*, p. 109.   [4] *Preaching*, p. 12.

return [shall be] to consummate the new Age.'[1] But most important of all Paul's expectations was that of a speedy return. This was also Paul's heritage from the primitive Church, for, as Professor Dodd observes, 'the expectation of a *speedy* advent must have had extraordinarily deep roots in Christian belief.'[2] 'Although Paul had already waited at least fifteen years since his conversion, yet in his earliest letters he is still expecting the Advent almost immediately.'[3] But in subsequent letters Professor Dodd detects a change in Paul's attitude toward a speedy return. 1 Corinthians still looks for the return in Paul's lifetime but in 2 Corinthians 'he has faced the fact that it is possible or probable that he will "go to stay with the Lord" through death'.[4] Finally, in Rom. 13.11-14 the same idea as 1 Thess. 5.1-11 is treated calmly without the former expectation of a return '*at any moment*'.[5] Paul seems to be changing his mind.

This change of attitude toward the expectation of the second advent plays a large role in Professor Dodd's argument. He gives to it as much weight as possible. In order to do so the early Church is pictured as obsessed with the idea of a speedy return and greatly shaken by the delay. God's plan 'now trembled upon the verge of its conclusion in His second advent. . . . As time went on, the indivisible unity of experience which lay behind the preaching of the apostles was broken. . . . The consequent demand for readjustment was a principal cause of the development of early Christian thought.'[6] This is no doubt in some measure true, but at this point there is need for caution against hasty conclusions. Paul no doubt adjusted his expectations from a speedy return to a simply imminent return, allowing the question of 'when' to drop. This amounted to taking seriously the answer of Christ to His disciples: 'But of that day or that hour no one knows, not even the angels in heaven, nor the Son, but only the Father. Take heed, watch; for you do not know when the time will come' (Mark 13.32-3). The alternatives were not, in Paul's mind, either a speedy return or disinterest in any return. Professor Dodd does not state expressly that Paul lost interest in the second advent of Christ, but he is in danger of implying as much. The implication is

[1] op. cit., p. 26.
[2] op. cit., p. 31. In *Scriptures*, p. 67, Professor Dodd points out that Dan. 7.13 was background material for the 'article of the *kerygma* which referred to the return of Christ as Judge and Saviour'.   [3] *Studies*, p. 109.
[4] op. cit., p. 110.   [5] op. cit., p. 111.   [6] *Preaching*, pp. 34, 35.

that the interest which Paul had lavished on a speedy return was subsequently shifted to an eschatological evaluation of events which had already taken place. The point to keep clearly in mind is that Paul's interest in these events was never lacking and that he always agreed with the earliest *kerygma* in an eschatological evaluation of these events.[1] There is no evidence that this evaluation only followed for Paul or any of the other New Testament writers because of a disappointment with regard to a speedy return. According to the earliest *kerygma* the Cross and resurrection of Christ were always at the centre of primitive Christian thought. With this reservation in mind we turn to Professor Dodd's description of the later Paul.

'The exposure of the illusion which fixed an early date for the Lord's advent, while it threw some minds back into the unwholesome ferment of apocalyptic speculation, gave to finer minds the occasion for grasping more firmly the substantive truths of the Gospel, and finding for them a more adequate expression.'[2] Paul abandons the 'futurist eschatology' of 2 Thess. 1.7-10 for 'realised eschatology'.[3] Paul 'says that in the death of Christ God manifested His righteousness and condemned sin in the flesh', and since 'the manifestation of righteousness and the condemnation of sin are functions of the Last Judgment, Professor Dodd implies that for the later Paul the Last Judgment took place at the Cross.[4] The later Paul came to believe 'that all that prophecy and apocalypse had asserted of the supernatural Messianic community was fulfilled in the Church'.[5] This was accomplished through his Christ-mysticism which unites the believer to the risen Christ and thereby gives the believer participation in His righteousness, holiness, glory and immortality in the communion of His body.[6] Professor Dodd goes so far as to say that for New Testament writers in general, 'the characteristics of the Day of the Lord as described in prophecy and apocalypse are boldly transferred to the historical

---

[1] In Professor Dodd's first summary of the early *kerygma* the eschatological evaluation is already evident. See the six points in *Preaching*, pp. 21-3.

[2] *Preaching*, p. 41.
[3] op. cit., p. 39.
[4] op. cit., p. 42.
[5] op. cit., p. 62.
[6] op. cit., p. 63. In the earlier treatment of the subject Professor Dodd fails to distinguish between a speedy return and an imminent return. Paul never wavered in the expectation of an imminent return. Thus it is not quite accurate to say that 'side by side with a diminishing emphasis on the imminence of the Advent goes a growing emphasis on the eternal life here and now in communion with Christ'. *Studies*, p. 113.

crisis [of the ministry, the death, and the resurrection of Jesus Christ]'.[1]

While Professor Dodd submits that the later Paul transferred his interest in the future to the ministry, the death, and the resurrection of Christ, and saw the fulfilment of the life of the 'Age to Come' in the Church's present life, he has to admit, in such phrases as 'the hope of glory yet to come remains as a background of thought',[2] or 'in its final form, it is true, the consummation of life is still a matter of hope,'[3] that Paul's interest in the future continues to stick out. In fact, an examination of the eschatology of the later Paul represented in Romans shows that he maintained a lively interest in the future, with its wrath, judgment, consummation, and completed work of the Spirit.

Professor Dodd's commentary on Romans makes it possible to examine in detail how well the later Paul fits his scheme of realised eschatology. Although *Romans* was the first of Professor Dodd's works to be published, it attempts to reinterpret, minimise or ignore the passages which refer to the future as though in preparation for the theory of realised eschatology which appeared three years later.

At the time when Paul wrote 2 Thess. 2 it is clear that the 'day of the Lord' with its accompanying judgment and second advent was still outstanding. Realised eschatology seeks to identify the 'day of the Lord' with the events of Christ's ministry, death, and resurrection and to exhaust divine judgment in historical consequences of sinfulness. 'The divine judgment is not a bare sentence, or expression of opinion. It is historical action.'[4] The Jewish War and World War I are suggested as examples of this historical judgment. In criticism it must be said that with Paul, also, the judgment of God is no mere expression of opinion. But according to Rom. 2 the execution of that judgment is reserved for the *future* as an expression of God's wrath, and is not fulfilled in the ordinary events of history. This 'day of wrath' is obviously in the future for Paul (Rom. 2.5, 6, 8, 9, 16). Professor Dodd attempts unsuccessfully to reinterpret 'wrath' as something realised in historical action. To begin with, in commenting on Rom. 1.18 he seeks altogether to avoid

---

[1] *Preaching*, p. 85. Still speaking of 'New Testament writers in general', he says, 'The implication is that . . . all that the prophets meant by the Day of the Lord is realised.' *Preaching*, p. 87.

[2] *Preaching*, p. 63.   [3] op. cit., p. 65.   [4] *History*, p. 173.

wrath as an attitude of God by citing all the passages which do not attribute anger to God. Then after dissociating wrath from God he reinterprets it as 'an inevitable process of cause and effect in a moral universe' illustrated by the process described in the concluding section of Rom. 1.[1] This recalls a statement of Professor Dodd in the introduction. 'Sometimes I think Paul is wrong, and I have ventured to say so.'[2] This is evidently one of those times, for here citations from other portions of the New Testament are played off against Rom. 1.18 in an attempt to show that anger could not be an attribute of God and that Paul is mistaken. This is a legitimate procedure for a commentator according to Professor Dodd's introduction, but for our present discussion it avoids the point, which is to see what Paul's eschatology was at the time when he wrote *Romans*.

In commenting on Rom. 2.5ff, Professor Dodd admits that 'the description of rewards and punishments which follows shows that Paul here has in view the traditional Day of Judgment, when the revelation of the Wrath will be complete. This is in accord with the eschatology which primitive Christianity inherited from Judaism, and his Jewish hearers would recognise it at once.'[3] Here is an express admission that Paul's eschatology has not become 'realised' in Rom. 2. It is amazing, in the light of this, that Professor Dodd still attempts to claim Paul for realised eschatology in Rom. 1. He does so only by attributing to Paul an eschatological view which contradicts Paul's own expression on the subject! The only point which seems to favour Professor Dodd's interpretation is the present tense of the verb 'reveal' in Rom. 1.18. But when taken together with 2.5, which puts the 'day of wrath' definitely also in the future, the meaning becomes clear. The wrath of God is His anger with sinners, His present attitude toward those who reject the knowledge of Him. (This idea of wrath Professor Dodd rejects.) How do we know God is angry with sinners, and how is His attitude now being revealed? Paul answers by pointing to the moral degradation of idolatry. This degradation, described in 1.18-32, is not exhibited as the execution of the sentence of judgment God's anger implies, but simply as a revelation of the fact that God is now angry because of sin. The implementing of this wrath in judgment is quite another thing from its being

---

[1] *Romans*, p. 23. 'It is the principle of retribution inherent in a moral universe.' *Romans*, p. 200.   [2] op. cit., p. xxxv.   [3] op. cit., p. xxxiii.

revealed, which is reserved for the future day of judgment described in 2.5ff. Surely an exegesis of Rom. 1.18-2.16 which shows a unity and progression in Paul's thought is preferable to Professor Dodd's explanation, which makes Paul think one way in Rom. 1 and another way in Rom. 2. From this consideration of wrath and judgment, it is clear that the Paul of *Romans*, the later Paul, does not belong to the camp of realised eschatology. It is equally clear that Paul regards as imminent the salvation which for the faithful accompanies the coming of the Day of the Lord.

Professor Dodd points out the parallel between Rom. 13.11-13 and 1 Thess. 5.4-8. In both passages, Paul is thinking of time in the same linear terms, and pleads for readiness for the day of salvation, which is drawing near and may come at any time. The only argument Professor Dodd can offer against this clear evidence of Paul's unchanged eschatology is the unsupported assertion that 'the eschatology has become little more than an imaginative expression for the urgency which belongs to all moral effort when it is thought of in relation to the eternal issues of life'.[1] In fact *Romans* shows that the 'later' Paul has lively hopes for the future. There is no evidence that his interest in the future has to be transferred to the present.

Paul looks forward also to eternal life, for with him salvation belongs ultimately to the future, as Rom. 13.11 indicates. Paul's use of 'eternal life' in 5.21 and 6.22-3 shows that for him the full benefits of salvation come in the next life. Professor Dodd avoids this futurist interest of Paul by simply overlooking these verses without commenting at all. In commenting on 8.5-13 Professor Dodd admits that Paul has a doctrine of immortality which is 'a distinctively Christian contribution to the problem of a future life'.[2] Rom. 8.11 also shows that Paul looks forward to life after death.

At the time when Paul wrote to the Romans he was looking forward to 'the redemption of our bodies', also in the future (8.23f). As shown by 8.24, 25, this is a hope which has been in no sense fulfilled in the present. For, as Paul explains, 'hope that is seen is not hope'. In his comment on these verses, Professor Dodd overlooks this futurist element by classing 'hope' with faith and love 'as one of the things that "abide"'.[3]

Paul's hope for the redemption of the body is a part of his

---

[1] *Romans*, p. 210.   [2] op. cit., p. 126.   [3] op. cit., p. 135.

broader hope for all creation that it should one day 'be set free from its bondage to decay' (Rom. 8.18-23). In view of these verses Professor Dodd has to admit that Paul 'shared with many of his contemporaries the belief that, in the Good Time Coming the material universe would be transfigured into a substance consisting of pure light or glory, thus returning to its original perfection as created by God'.[1] Here again is further proof that Paul's interest in the future has not been transferred to present events.

In commenting on Rom. 8.14-17, Professor Dodd well brings out Paul's expectation of future glorification and the Spirit's present work as a pledge of this future benefit. 'The "inheritance" is the future blessedness of perfect existence; but already we possess (Eph. 1.14) "the pledge and instalment of our common heritage", in possessing the Spirit. . . . And so Paul's thought is turned, more definitely and emphatically than before, from the present to the glorious future at which he had hinted in 6.5, 8.11.'[2] Unfortunately, Professor Dodd is not always so consistent in his relating of the Spirit to the future. When he comes elsewhere to draw out the meaning of Paul's doctrine of the Spirit as the *arrhabon* his Platonic presuppositions do not hinder him from noting that 'in its final form, it is true, the consummation of life is still a matter of hope, but the earnest (*arrhabon*) of the inheritance is a present possession; and an *arrhabon* is a first instalment of a sum due accepted as a guarantee for the payment of the whole'.[3] But in his otherwise excellent, concise sketch of the word 'spirit' he cannot appreciate its futuristic aspect.[4] He recognises the Spirit 'as the supernatural or divine element breaking into human life' and as 'proof (for Christians) that they were living in a new age, inaugurated by the resurrection of Christ', but fails to see that this new age is only come in a measure, and that the Spirit who now dispenses in a preliminary way some of the benefits of the new age will in the future implement that new age in all its glory. All these examples from *Romans* show that Paul, contrary to Professor Dodd, had not shifted his interest from the future to the present.

Conclusion

The main fallacy in Professor Dodd's argument for realised

[1] op. cit., p. 134.   [2] op. cit., p. 132.   [3] *Preaching*, p. 65.   [4] *Romans*, pp. 116-18.

eschatology in Paul seems to be that in noting the change from belief in a speedy return of Christ to belief in an imminent return of Christ he has attempted to prove too much. He has been able to do no more than to demonstrate a change in Paul's thought which in his own words seems 'not of great importance', a change which in reality is 'merely a readjustment, so to speak, of the eschatological time-table'.[1] We have been able to show from Romans that Paul continued to hold futuristic and apocalyptic elements as an integral part of his theology. Professor Dodd's commentary could not dispense with them. Hope for the future continued to play a positive role in his thought well into his mature life. Furthermore, these futuristic elements in Paul's writings show that the Platonic concept of time does not fit the Apostle's thought. Perhaps Professor Dodd makes a better case for it in John's *Gospel* and Hebrews. That is not here for us to judge. But in Paul the linear conception of time fits the facts best.

Because of the intrusion of Platonic elements into Professor Dodd's exposition of Paul it seems to me that he has missed the true nature of the eschatological tension in Paul. In realised eschatology the tension is between the absolute and the relative, while in Paul the tension is that between the already-present and the not-yet-fulfilled. It is a temporal, not a metaphysical tension.

In the light of these conclusions the argument behind the development of Paul's doctrine of the Holy Spirit and eschatology, Chs. I-III does not seem to be invalidated by the claims of realised eschatology.

Apart from what seem to be the inaccuracies in realised eschatology, upon which unfortunately it has been the business of this chapter to dwell, it has many strong points to commend it. Realised eschatology places the centre of *Heilsgeschichte* squarely in the proper place at the ministry, the cross, and the resurrection of Christ. By placing the emphasis on God's acts and God's initiative it has disposed of the idea of automatic progress as a possible Christian interpretation of history. It recognises through its choice of the centre of revelation the Christocentric nature of the Spirit. And finally it draws attention to the benefits of redemption which are available and active now.

[1] *Studies*, p. 112.

VI

RUDOLF BULTMANN'S REINTERPRETED ESCHATOLOGY

1. *Paul's Doctrine*

PROFESSOR BULTMANN's study of the New Testament has led him into a difficult but not unfamiliar situation. After careful analysis of the content of the New Testament documents he finds himself unable to accept that content, unable to believe in the Biblical witness as it stands. This is no unfamiliar situation, since it was this dilemma which, we have seen, led Dr Schweizer to reject the New Testament teaching as obsolete. To a lesser degree it troubled Professor Dodd, so that he had to select those elements out of the New Testament which he found acceptable in accordance with his preference for the realised aspects of eschatology. Professor Bultmann preserves the validity and relevance of the content of the New Testament by a thorough reinterpretation.

Before the application of this reinterpretation, Professor Bultmann carefully expounds the content of the documents. There can be no doubt that he has an unusual talent for grasping their content and giving it back again in an orderly and concise fashion. And where his reinterpretation does not creep in, his exposition of the Holy Spirit's relation to eschatology, so far as it goes, agrees essentially with the conclusions reached in Chs. I-III above. Professor Bultmann's treatment of the Spirit in Paul is given partly in his treatment of the *kerygma* of the Hellenistic Church, because he reckons Paul among the Hellenists in primitive Christianity, but also in his treatment of Pauline theology in his *Theology of the New Testament*.[1]

---

[1] The following works will be cited according to their corresponding abbreviations:

(a)   *Offenbarung*=*Der Begriff der Offenbarung im Neuen Testament*, 1929.
(b)   *Critics*='Bultmann replies to his Critics', in *Kerygma and Myth*, ed. Hans Werner Bartsch, London 1953, pp. 191-211.
(c)   *Geschichtlichkeit*='Die Geschichtlichkeit des Daseins und der Glaube', in *Zeitschrift fuer Theologie und Kirche*, Tübingen, XI (1930), pp. 339-64.
(d)   *Mythology*—'New Testament and Mythology', in *Kerygma and Myth*, pp. 1-44.

He begins with a general definition of the Spirit. 'This, then, constitutes the concept of *pneuma*: it is the miraculous—in so far as that takes place in the sphere of human life—either in what men do or what is done to them.'[1] Then follows an enumeration of the various gifts attributed to the Spirit. There is no special presentation of the Spirit in relation to Christ. (Later in the chapter we shall attempt to account for this.) 'According to Paul it [the Spirit] is above all the power for ethical living'—an idea peculiar to Paul.[2] The Spirit is the norm of the earthly 'walk' of the man of faith.[3]

Professor Bultmann recognises the eschatology of Paul for what it is. 'He holds fast to the traditional-Jewish-Christian teaching of the resurrection of the dead, and in so doing he also retains the apocalyptic expectation of the last judgment and of the cosmic drama which will end the old world and introduce the new world of salvation, "that which is perfect" (1 Cor. 13.10). He expects the "day" (or the "coming"—*parousia*) of the "Lord" (1 Cor. 1.8, 5.5, 15.23; 2 Cor. 1.14; Phil. 1.6, 10, 2.16; 1 Thess. 2.19, 3.13, 4.15, 5.2, 23), which will also be the end of this reign, which began with the resurrection, and the dawn of the period of salvation, in which God will be all in all (1 Cor. 15.24-7).'[4] Thus Professor Bultmann recognises that for Paul salvation is primarily a future thing, though he notices that eschatological righteousness is already present. Christians may hope on the basis of the Spirit-given knowledge of God's 'love'.[5] This introduces us to the relation of the Spirit to eschatology.

'The "bodily" resurrection' is 'the transformation of the *soma* from under the power of flesh into a spiritual *soma*, i.e. a Spirit-ruled soma.'[6] In fact the gift of the Spirit was itself an eschatological sign. 'For Paul, the Spirit at work in the Church was the first-fruits (Rom. 8.23) or the guarantee (2 Cor. 1.22, 5.5) of the imminent fulfilment, so that the earliest Church knew that it had been given *the Spirit*, that gift of the end of days

(e)   Schniewind = 'A Reply to the Theses of J. Schniewind', in *Kerygma and Myth*, pp. 102-123.
(f)   *Theology* = *Theology of the New Testament*, London 1952, VOL. I.
[1] *Theology*, p. 154.   [2] op. cit., p. 157.   [3] op. cit., p. 336.
[4] op. cit., p. 346. But elsewhere it is claimed that Paul has modified traditional eschatology until it fits better Bultmann's own view, e.g.—'In Paul history is swallowed up in eschatology. Thereby eschatology has wholly lost its sense as goal of history and is in fact understood as the goal of the individual human being.' Bultmann, 'History and Eschatology in the New Testament', in *NT Studies*, 1 (1954), p. 13.
[5] *Theology*, p. 347.   [6] op. cit., p. 201.

which, according to the Jewish view, had departed from Israel with the last of the prophets, but whose impartation [sic] was promised for the end of days.'[1] 'The bestowal of the Spirit is an eschatological gift and . . . its coming into the Church is an eschatological event.'[2] Thus possession of the Spirit 'lends the assurance of triumph over death, the certainty of the resurrection and of eternal life'.[3]

Professor Bultmann does not relate the Spirit so definitely to the future as in Ch. II above, nor does he trace out the working of the Spirit in terms of fulfilled and outstanding aspects of that working as in Ch. III; but he does recognise the characteristic time-tension of the present. He refers to 'the paradox of the Christian situation . . . which Paul characterises as the situation between "no longer" and "not yet" (Phil. 3.12-14).'[4] 'We are what we are in hope. For that is the other side of the Christian situation: though Christian existence can, on the one hand, be described by the indicatives—we are sanctified, we are purified—nevertheless, so long as it moves within this world, it stands under the imperative.'[5] And this paradoxical nature of the Christian situation is characteristic of, and a result of, the working of the Spirit. ' "Life" already actualises itself in the present, for he who is baptised has received the gift of the Spirit as the "first-fruits" or "guarantee" of future salvation' (Rom. 8.23; 2 Cor. 1.22; 5.5).[6]

2. *Bultmann's Problem*

But in this otherwise Pauline doctrine there appears, now and then, a concern to correct tendencies in Paul with which Professor Bultmann does not seem to be quite satisfied. For example, he wants to bring out clearly that action of the Spirit upon a man does not detract from the man's responsibility. 'Freedom and demand constitute a unity. Only when this unity is understood, is Paul's thought of the Spirit understood aright—and that means: when the Spirit is conceived of not as a mysterious power working with magical compulsion. . . .'[7]

[1] op. cit., p. 41.   [2] op. cit., p. 155.   [3] op. cit., p. 157.   [4] op. cit., p. 100.
[5] op. cit., p. 101. 'The baptised Christian who, as such, belongs to the world to come, is, in his temporary present existence, not yet what he is to be and in the sight of God already is, but that his belonging to the world to come nevertheless determines his present existence' (p. 163).
[6] op. cit., p. 348.
[7] op. cit., p. 336. The same concern against the view of the Spirit as 'a magically [mechanically] working power' is expressed on p. 163.

(Behind Professor Bultmann's distinction beween two modes of
the Spirit's operation, might there lie an objection to the miraculous?) 'On the one hand, it is the power conferred in baptism
which makes the Christian a Christian. . . . On the other hand,
it is the power given now and again for the occasion to the
Christian, enabling him to accomplish extraordinary things.'[1]
Finally, in speaking of the relation of the Spirit to the resurrection body Professor Bultmann comes right out with it. There
are some things about Paul's doctrine he just cannot accept.
'Since Paul's capacity for abstract thinking is not a developed
one, and he therefore does not distinguish terminologically between *soma* in the basic sense of that which characterises human
existence and *soma* as the phenomenon of the material body,
he connects the idea of somatic existence in the eschatological
consummation with a mythological teaching on the resurrection
(1 Cor. 15). In it *soma* must appear somehow or other as a
thing of material substance, or as the "form" of such a thing.
And since the substance of the resurrection body cannot be
"flesh and blood" (1 Cor. 15.50), the unfortunate consequence
is that *pneuma* must be conceived as a substance of which that
soma consists.'[2] It is extremely important to note that the unacceptable element in Paul's thought is called 'mythological'.
This is what makes Paul's doctrines, as they stand, unacceptable
to Professor Bultmann. As we have noted, he has carefully
studied the content of the New Testament and found it unacceptable. What are the unacceptable things about Paul's
doctrine of the Holy Spirit and eschatology?

In the first place, Professor Bultmann had defined the Spirit
in Paul as the miraculous in the sphere of human life. This
'miracle' element belongs to an obsolete mythological view of
the world according to Professor Bultmann. 'The miracles of
the New Testament have ceased to be miraculous.'[3]

In the second place, the basic concept of *pneuma* is itself
unacceptable. He finds that 'what the New Testament has to
say about the "Spirit" . . . utterly strange and incomprehensible. Biological man cannot see how a supernatural entity
like the *pneuma* can penetrate within the close texture of his
natural powers and set to work in him.'[4] This is what was
behind the above-mentioned concern about the eclipse of man's

[1] op. cit., p. 162.   [2] op. cit., pp. 198, 199.
[3] *Mythology*, p. 5.   [4] op. cit., p. 6.

74

responsibility. The modern conception of human nature is that it is 'a self-subsistent unity immune from the interference of supernatural powers'.[1]

Thirdly, Paul's eschatology will not do. 'We can no longer look for the return of the Son of Man on the clouds of heaven or hope that the faithful will meet him in the air' (1 Thess. 4.15ff).[2] 'The mythical eschatology is untenable for the simple reason that the *parousia* of Christ never took place as the New Testament expected. History did not come to an end, and, as every schoolboy knows, it will continue to run its course. Even if we believe that the world as we know it will come to an end in time, we expect the end to take the form of a natural catastrophe, not of a mythical event such as the New Testament expects.'[3] These three objections leave little of the original Pauline doctrine intact. In a candid sentence Professor Bultmann reveals that his objections to the mythological are personal. 'For my part, the only interpretation I can give to the Pauline . . . eschatology is a critical one.'[4] When Professor Bultmann speaks of the difficulties of the 'modern man' with the New Testament it seems to me clear that he is speaking autobiographically. This is for Professor Bultmann a very real and personal problem. He is no doubt correct in believing that others share this difficulty with him. What is to be done? Whatever the solution, a great service has been done by bringing this question so starkly to the attention of Biblical scholarship. Perhaps the sharp formulation of the question rather than the answer he gives is Professor Bultmann's main contribution.

Three possible solutions to this problem present themselves. The Biblical witness may be completely rejected as obsolete. This solution of 'the liberal theologians of the last century' Professor Bultmann rejects because 'they threw away not only the mythology but also the *kerygma* itself'.[5] Then may we eliminate certain objectionable features and keep the rest? No, this solution is also unsatisfactory. 'Whatever else may be true, we cannot save the *kerygma* by selecting some of its features and subtracting others, and thus reduce the amount of mythology in it.'[6] Obviously, Professor Bultmann cannot simply accept the whole naively, so that the only possible solution is a thorough reinterpretation of the New Testament. What he remarks

---

[1] op. cit., p. 7.   [2] op. cit., p. 4.   [3] op. cit., p. 5.
[4] *Schniewind*, p. 116.   [5] *Mythology*, p. 12.   [6] op. cit., p. 9.

concerning Paul's use of *pneuma* describes his intended solution of all Paul's thought. 'In distinction from this mythology the real intention of Paul must be made clear.'[1] Professor Bultmann is convinced that Paul is saying something through mythology that is worth our attention. How may we distil out this 'real intention'? Upon what lines may this reinterpretation proceed? Professor Bultmann has a very definite answer.

3. *The Reinterpretation*

The name which has become popular for this reinterpretation is 'demythologising'. 'The *kerygma* is incredible to modern man, for he is convinced that the mythological view of the world is obsolete.'[2] Yet mythology expresses something that is still valid, for 'the real purpose of myth is not to present an objective picture of the world as it is, but to express man's understanding of himself in the world in which he lives. Myth should be interpreted not cosmologically, but anthropologically. . . .'[3] In other words, men are men in all times and places. Whatever their understanding of the objective world around them, the situation remains the same. Thus, if Paul had a valid understanding of the human situation in his time, that same understanding will be valid for our time. The task then is to decipher his language, his mythology, his world view, and penetrate to his self-understanding. The advantage of such a hermeneutics is obvious. Although Paul's statements about the nature of man's environment are not true, yet in a deeper sense everything he says may be true of the human situation. From this point of view Paul is relevant and valid for every age. The Biblical witness is vindicated—provided one can accept the fact that the authoritative kernel of Paul's thought is merely his self-understanding.

At this crucial point in Professor Bultmann's programme, his solution is open to serious question. This is of course a departure from the Church's attitude towards the witness of the Bible. The Biblical world view must be open to correction from empirical science. But when Paul speaks of realms beyond the reach of the laboratory instruments of empirical science, it has been the custom of the Church to accept that witness as true. It is difficult to see why modern scientific man has an advantage over Paul when the matters under discussion are extra-scientific.

---

[1] *Theology*, p. 198.   [2] *Mythology*, p. 3.   [3] op. cit., p. 10.

Nevertheless all that is important about Paul when Professor Bultmann considers him is his self-understanding. After all, what was his conversion? 'In it he surrendered his previous understanding of himself . . .' for a new self-understanding.[1]

But how do we know after all that Paul's self-understanding was valid? This is a matter of faith. We *believe* that the New Testament enshrines a true understanding of existence.

Once Professor Bultmann has laid out the general direction of his solution there is still much to be done. There needs to be a key to decipher the cryptography of mythology in order to get at Paul's understanding of human existence. What is the basic structure of human existence valid for all times? This key Professor Bultmann is satisfied that he has found in the existentialist philosophy of Martin Heidegger.

It has been objected that at this point Professor Bultmann imports extra-Biblical norms from philosophy and thus subordinates theology to philosophy. This is not Professor Bultmann's opinion, because for him theology and philosophy have a legitimate common ground as well as their own distinct areas. 'Philosophy and theology have the same object, human existence, but they make a theme of it in different ways. Philosophy makes a theme out of the *being* of human existence, in that it investigates the formal structures of human existence ontologically (scientifically, in philosophical terms). Theology speaks of concrete human existence in so far as it believes (or does not believe, which is for it not something negative but something positive), in so far as its "how" is characterised by being met (or as the "how" of human existence ought to be met) by a definite proclamation.'[2] Philosophy alone gives theology 'the possibility of understanding conceptually such terms as "proclamation", "word", "address", "hearing", without ever teaching it to understand a concrete proclamation.'[3]

Receiving a terminology and an understanding of the structure of human existence from philosophy is no eclipse of revelation for Professor Bultmann, because revelation is not concerned with the structure of human existence as such. The purpose of revelation is to give a man a particular understanding of himself, i.e. the understanding of himself which faith gives. 'The question about revelation is the question about the limitation of a person; and the answer to the question what revelation

[1] *Theology*, p. 188.   [2] *Geschichtlichkeit*, p. 343.   [3] op. cit., pp. 340, 341.

77

is can be received only when the inquirer is ready to let his limitation be uncovered.'[1] 'Revelation is not enlightenment, the communication of knowledge.'[2]

It remains to be seen now what results when these ideas are applied to Paul's doctrine of the Spirit and eschatology. Incidentally, Professor Bultmann does not pretend to have carried out the reinterpretation, the demythologising, of the New Testament. This task 'will tax the time and strength of a whole theological generation'.[3] But he has gone far enough himself to indicate the nature of the results. The 'real intention' of Paul turns out to be startlingly different from what he simply *says*. Professor Bultmann's reinterpretation amounts to a transformation.

Remembering that 'the importance of the New Testament mythology lies not in its imagery but in the understanding of existence which it enshrines', we first consider the reinterpretation of Paul's eschatological 'imagery'.[4] From Professor Bultmann's point of view 'the only true interpretation of eschatology is one which makes it a real experience of human life'.[5] The basic reference of the word eschatology is reinterpreted. The idea of some end is not essential. 'The essential thing about the eschatological message is the idea of God that operates in it and the idea of human existence that it contains—not the belief that the end of the world is just ahead.'[6] 'I do not see why it is necessary to think of a temporal end of time'.[7] In its reinterpreted form 'eschatological' comes to mean 'other than this world', i.e. a determination of existence other than that of the world. It means 'a life based on invisible, intangible realities'.[8] This reinterpretation of eschatology corresponds to Heidegger's idea of death in his analysis of human existence, for the essential idea behind both death and eschatology is man's limitedness (*Begrenztheit*). 'Man is bounded by death.'[9] Corresponding to this idea that 'eschatological' is that 'in which the world finds its end', is the concept of the new man.[10] Thus eschatological existence means being a 'new creature'.[11]

The closely related ideas of time and history are similarly transformed. Past, present, and future are no longer connected on a time-line. Past has practically no reality except in the

[1] *Offenbarung*, p. 12.
[2] op. cit., p. 29.
[3] *Mythology*, p. 15.
[4] op. cit., p. 11.
[5] *Schniewind*, p. 106.
[6] *Theology*, p. 23.
[7] *Schniewind*, p. 118.
[8] op. cit., p. 113.
[9] *Offenbarung*, p. 20.
[10] op. cit., p. 30.
[11] *Mythology*, p. 20.

measure in which it can be made present. 'As a past fact the Cross cannot be an event in our lives' but 'the unique event of past history (the Cross) is an ever-present reality.'[1] (This making present of the past is achieved in preaching.[2]) Thus the past and present are for faith blended together in a timeless now. Yet Professor Bultmann is 'surprised how readily people conclude that my interpretation of the New Testament eschatology implies a timeless "now"', and yet the only alternative he offers is the ambiguous statement that 'the now of the New Testament is both timeless and temporal'.[3] To match this negation of the past, the New Testament meaning of *ephapax* 'once for all time' is replaced with the idea of the events of redemptive history happening 'once at a time' or 'time after time' in human encounters. *Ephapax* 'does not mean the datable uniqueness and finality of an event of past history, but teaches us in a high degree of paradox to believe that just such an event of the past is the once-and-for-all eschatological event, which is continually re-enacted in the word of proclamation.'[4]

This has the effect of cancelling out the historical basis for the relation between the Spirit and Christ. If the Cross is not a permanent event of the past, then the Spirit was not poured out as a result of Christ's work. Nor can we conclude anything about the nature and work of the Spirit from the role of the Spirit in the resurrection and in the exalted Lord's resurrected manner of existence. This is so because 'the resurrection itself is not an event of past history. If the event of Easter Day is in any sense an historical event additional to the event of the Cross, it is nothing else than the rise of faith in the risen Lord. . . .'[5] If the resurrection and the resurrection mode of existence are products of faith they cannot provide material which can inform faith. That would be to believe something because one told it to oneself. Perhaps this underlies the fact that Professor Bultmann discusses the Christocentric nature of the Spirit neither in his exposition nor in his reinterpretation of Paul's thought.

Professor Bultmann's reinterpretation dissolves the past into the present, but what becomes of the future? It receives some

---

[1] *Schniewind*, pp. 110, 111. [2] *Offenbarung*, p. 30. [3] *Schniewind*, p. 114.
[4] *Critics*, p. 209. *Schniewind*, p. 115, 'the Now of the New Testament implies that the supra-temporal reality becomes an event for each particular individual only by virtue of an encounter in time.'
[5] *Mythology*, p. 42.

of the weight taken from the past, for in Heidegger's analysis (after which Professor Bultmann patterns his reinterpretation), the future is of tremendous importance. Again the future is not the 'not yet' of a succession of 'nows' on a time-line. It is human existence moving forward in resolve toward its possibilities.[1] Before faith, a man's future, i.e. his field of possibilities, was bounded by death. But through faith he is freed from death. 'Freedom from death means possessing genuine future, whereas man under the power of death, as he formerly was, had no future.'[2] In this statement it is clear that Professor Bultmann equates the future with the possibilities of existing in a certain way, i.e. the possibility of authentic existence.

This brings us to the reinterpreted doctrine of the Spirit in relation to the reinterpreted eschatology. It could be said that in his own way Professor Bultmann's new doctrine of the Spirit is bound up primarily with the future, as argued above in Ch. II. He identifies the Spirit with the future. For he explains the gift of the Spirit to mean that the believer 'has been given freedom—freedom from the power of sin and death'.[3] But this is, as we have just seen above, the same as saying that the gift of the Spirit means that a man possesses a genuine future. The result is that the Spirit becomes nothing but the description of the situation of the man of faith with his possibility of authentic existence. The Spirit does not have a *relation* to the future. The Spirit is *replaced* by the future. In the last analysis future and Spirit are merely descriptions of a particular manner of human existence. The objective reality of the Spirit disappears! 'In the last resort he [Paul] clearly means by "Spirit" the possibility of a new life which is opened up by faith. The Spirit does not work like a supernatural force, nor is it the permanent possession of the believer.'[4] For, in fact, the Spirit is not anything.

One more aspect of the reinterpretation of Paul remains to be investigated. Let us compare it with the exegesis of Ch. III, which found a temporal tension between 'already' and 'not yet' to be characteristic of the action of the Spirit in the Christian's life. Though actually for him the role of the Spirit is gone, Professor Bultmann describes this situation just as we have done. 'To believe . . . means to be travelling along the road between

---

[1] For a summary of Heidegger's ideas of future, past, and present, see Brock, introduction to Heidegger, *Existence and Being*, pp. 9ff.
[2] *Theology*, p. 332.　　　　[3] op. cit., p. 333.　　　　[4] *Mythology*, p. 22.

the "already" and the "not yet", always to be pursuing a goal.'[1]
But this does not imply that that goal is the life of the coming
age. 'The age to come cannot be conceived as a further period
in history or as overlapping the old age like two epochs in history.'[2] For this would only be possible in the context of a time-
line which has disappeared in the reinterpretation.

4. *Conclusion*

Professor Bultmann possesses the kind of mind that evidently
abhors objective reality beyond the horizon of scientific materi-
alism. To make belief easier he reduces these transcendental,
supernatural entities to an absolute minimum. He finds it difficult, it seems, to believe in decisive acts in history and human
personality that originate in this transcendent realm. Heidegger's *Sein und Zeit* provided him with a philosophical structure
and terminology in sympathy with this abhorrence of the transcendent and metaphysical, for what Professor Bultmann wants
to do in theology, *Sein und Zeit* had already done in philosophy,
in the sense that, in his study of being Heidegger was primarily
concerned with the subjects, the self, the empirical, as the road
to the understanding of being. 'The fundamental criticism
which Heidegger advances against the whole European philo-
sophic tradition is that its "ontological" exposition was fundamentally concerned exclusively with what is *"vorhanden"* (the
things that are given by nature). . . .'[3] This is exactly Professor
Bultmann's criticism of theology. Adapted to his concern, the
same statement would be: The fundamental criticism which
Bultmann advances against the whole European theological
tradition is that its exposition of the nature of deity and the
realm of the Spirit was fundamentally concerned exclusively
with what is given as divine or created objective reality. The
result in the case of Professor Bultmann is to reduce time, the
eschatological age to come and the Spirit which is the agent of
that age, to merely subjective experiences of the 'man of faith'.

There would be no criticism of such a programme if the de-
clared intention were to depart from Pauline thought as a norm
for such a theology and on the basis of certain other presuppositions create a new theology. But to profess to exhibit in
such a theology the 'real intention' of Paul is claiming too much.

[1] op. cit., p. 21. [2] *Schniewind*, p. 114.
[3] Brock, introduction to Heidegger, *Existence and Being*.

It is obvious that Paul was not attempting to criticise, or where possible eliminate, the (to him and his fellow Christians), objective entities of the realm of the Spirit and substitute for them a descriptive psychology of the Christian community of his day. To have told him that the Spirit did not exist but was merely a description of his situation as a man of faith would probably have brought the same reaction as telling a married man that his wife is not 'there'—it just *seems* that way because of his particular understanding of himself.

Actually there is no basis for the comparison of the results of this study of Paul's doctrine of the Holy Spirit and eschatology and Professor Bultmann's reinterpretation of Paul, for his reinterpretation could hardly be called Pauline.

But even aside from his reinterpretation there is this basic difference between this exposition and Professor Bultmann's. He does not find it necessary to emphasise the Christological aspect of the Spirit. This is probably so for two reasons. First, the ministry, death and resurrection of Christ are not the kind of events that could in any forensic or historical way provide a basis for the Spirit's release and activity among believers. And second, it is understandable that he should not press the implications of Christology or eschatology for the doctrine of the Spirit, for in the back of his mind the Spirit is something that has no ultimate reality.

Professor Bultmann's contribution is not so much the exposition of Biblical thought as it is a challenging solution to the pressing need for a tenable, articulate Biblical hermeneutic. In this regard his work is invaluable—as a challenge.

VII

SUMMARY AND IMPLICATIONS

1. *Summary*

BEFORE TREATING the broader theological implications and conclusions of our study, let us refresh our memory with a brief review of the current of thought in the first three chapters. The point of Ch. I was to show that Paul's Christology is the primary basis for his doctrine of the Spirit. An examination of the five Pauline passages in which the Spirit is related most directly to Christ (2 Cor. 3.17, 1 Cor. 12.3, Rom. 8.9*b*, Gal. 4.6, Phil. 1.19) showed a most intimate connexion between the two. In 2 Cor. 3.17 they are identified. The nature of this identity became clear when we noted that the context presents the Spirit as the agent which mediates the benefits of the new covenant which are available in Christ. By virtue of the fact that the benefits are inseparable from Christ's person, the Spirit, in communicating the benefits of redemption, in effect communicates Christ. Thus from the standpoint of the believer receiving these benefits the Spirit and the Lord are one. This identity we have described as a dynamic one, which occurs as the Spirit carries out His redemptive action in and for the believer. This dynamic identity was seen to underlie the remaining four passages.

In another group of passages related to the resurrection-exaltation of Christ, (Rom. 1.4; 1 Cor. 6.14, 15.45) a further connexion between the Spirit and Christ was discovered. It was seen that the Spirit was the power which accomplished Christ's resurrection and the life principle of His new exaltation-existence. The resurrection and exaltation are but two sides of the one continuous act of the Spirit whereby Jesus was raised from death to the exaltation life of His Lordship. This explained the appropriateness of the role of the Spirit as the mediator of Christ's presence to the believer, since the Spirit is the new life of the exalted Lord.

In comparison with the other New Testament witnesses this

aspect of the Pauline view of the Spirit is most nearly like that of John. The dynamic identity of the Spirit and Christ resulting from the redemptive activity of the Spirit is concisely summed up in the ἄλλον of ἄλλον παράκλητον in John 14.16, which indicates that the Spirit will be a companion to the disciples, as Jesus has been during His earthly ministry. He will be 'another' Lord to them.

A further examination of Rom. 1.4 showed that Christ's resurrection is continuous with the future general resurrection of the end time. And this brought us to the main point of Ch. II, namely, that the other basis of Paul's pneumatology beside his Christology is his eschatology. In this chapter we discovered that the Spirit is related primarily to the future, to eternity, to the time of the consummation of the redemptive process. This was evident from the descriptions of the Spirit as 'first-fruits', 'beginning' and 'first-born' (1 Cor. 15.20, 23; Col. 1.18), which place the emphasis on the future and refer to the present activity of the Spirit as merely preliminary. Rom. 8.11 made it clear that the Spirit is to be the agent of the general resurrection. Then began an examination of the passages which showed the primary relation of the Spirit to the future—first those containing the term ἀρραβών (2 Cor. 1.22, 5.5; Eph. 1.14) and then those relating the Spirit to the Kingdom of God (Rom. 14.17, 1 Cor. 4.20). This second chapter concluded by showing how the future breaks into the present in Paul's eschatology.

In Ch. III we continued the discussion by combining the insights of the two preceding chapters to show how the Christological and eschatological aspects of Paul's doctrine of the Spirit determine his understanding of the nature of Christian life in the period between Christ's resurrection and the end. First we noted those passages which make it most obvious that the Spirit is at work in the believer and in the Church (2 Cor. 13.13, Phil. 2.2, Eph. 1.13, Rom. 8.9, 1 Cor. 3.16, Eph. 2.22, Rom. 8.9, 11). In fact it was seen that the Christian's life is altogether a product of the Christocentric, *eschaton*-related Spirit. Finally, particular aspects of Christian life and experience were examined to show how the future relates to the present, producing the tension which is peculiar to Christian existence in the present.

2. *Implications for a doctrine of Christian life*

In the Synoptics the Spirit is primarily the special equipment

84

granted to a chosen individual for the execution of a God-appointed mission. This is essentially a pre-Pentecost, Old Testament understanding of the work of the Spirit. Paul's view of the Spirit goes beyond this to a pneumatology appropriate to the era of the Christian Church. In its presentation of the Spirit as the agent which bridges the gap between the historical Jesus, the now resurrected and exalted Lord, and the believer who waits until He comes and receives him to Himself, John's doctrine of the Spirit is in harmony with Paul's. The Synoptic doctrine finds its continuation in Paul in the equipment of each member of the body of Christ with gifts to fulfil his appointed function. If it be realised that Paul's doctrine includes the essential facets of the New Testament witness regarding the Spirit, implications drawn from it may be credited with very broad theological validity.

At the outset of this study we had hoped to shed some light on the subject of the Christian life. There are at least two ways of regarding the Christian life which must be called into question if our conclusions are taken seriously. The first is that which sees the Christian life as an existence beyond the continual defilement of sin on condition that one takes the ethical demands of the gospel with ultimate seriousness and exerts oneself with a corresponding earnestness. For if a Christian but does his best, that is all that can be expected by God or man. And whatever is thereby left undone cannot reasonably be accounted as sin. The conscience is clear. There are many varieties of the view I am seeking to isolate—from a carefully worked-out sinless perfection which preserves justification by faith to a theologically naive moralism—but they all have this in common, that they issue in a quiet conscience without necessity for further confession of sin.

Evaluated from the point of view of our findings, this view must be called into question by its truncated doctrine of the Spirit. What is commendable in this view is its recognition that the Spirit is at work transforming and sanctifying life. The Christological side of pneumatology may be well appreciated. What is lacking in it is that it does not take account of the eschatological aspect of the Spirit's activity, or that, if it is considered at all the proper eschatological tension is dissolved in a realised eschatology. According to this view the present evil age is past for the believer, and he lives entirely in the age to come. But the times are not in our hands so to dispose. As a matter of fact the age to come is not yet come, except in a measure, and the present evil age is very much with us. There is no use ignoring or denying the fact that all humans are destined to share the mortality and defilement of the present era until the end comes. Then are we victims of circumstance and absolved from responsibility? No, for the circumstances, in so far as they are unfortunate, are of our own making—the present evil age is our own creation, and in so far as the circumstances are favourable they are of God's making—the breaking in of the power of the new age is strictly a gift. When seen correctly, the believers' predicament for the present is not one of complete deliverance from evil which issues in unbroken ethical achievement.

The second view of Christian life over against which we should like to define our own conclusions is one which recognises the constant presence of sin and corruption in human existence. At the same time it recognises the ethical imperative imbedded in the indicative of the gospel. But this ethical imperative is for the most part not susceptible of realisation and must be accommodated to the evil present in every situation of the man of faith. In this view the cry most typical of the Christian life is, 'I believe, help thou mine unbelief'. The Christian must live in two power realms, and to be realistic he should make the adjustment and render unto Caesar the things that are Caesar's and unto God the things that are God's. On occasion he must rise above principle. Ethical compromise is sometimes one's duty, in fact it is necessary if one is to participate effectively in the world.

The advantage of this view is that it leaves no other possible ground to stand on before God except justification by faith alone, since good works are practically non-existent. Its disadvantages are that it too easily adopts an attitude of despair as the normal mood of Christian life and that it leads to a double standard which tailors ethical imperatives to suit the possibilities of the human situation. In the light of our conclusions its basic error is to disregard the eschatological orientation of the activity of the Spirit who determines the nature of Christian existence. Since the break-in of the new age in the power of the Spirit, the present age has lost its rights to the believer. Sin and corruption can no longer claim to belong to his existence as an essential component. The world has no right now to expect his accommodation to it. Since the coming of the Spirit, the present age has been judged *passé*. To be realistic now means to adjust oneself to the new age. Not only has the pre-Spirit situation lost its rights to and its claims upon the believer, it has also lost some of its power. The Spirit already overcomes evil in a measure. Redemption deals not only with the guilt but also with the power of sin.

The view of Christian life which Paul's doctrine of the Spirit implies has three facets which taken together make it a distinctive whole. First, Christian existence is determined Christologically. The Spirit first performed His distinctively redemptive work in the resurrection and exaltation of Christ. As a result of Christ's death and resurrection the Spirit has come upon believers to bestow this resurrection life of Christ, and to remove them from the power of sin and death. Thus Christian existence is something outside of and foreign to man which comes to him as a gift. It can only be understood as Christ's life, for here is its source and pattern. This life of a believer is still only a preliminary and indistinct copy of the original. As a result Christian existence is a life of gratitude to and union with Christ.

The second facet which characterises Christian life is the fact that the Spirit who is the life principle of the new age of consummation has been given. The Christian life is one of consummation, fulfilment, participation in the benefits of redemption. Because the new age has made itself felt, the Christian experiences spiritual growth, ethical victory, a sloughing off of sins, an exercising of gifts to the strengthening of the Church, and obedience to God. These things belong to the the life of the Christian. They make Christian existence a life of joy and victory.

Finally, Christian life is characterised by the fact that the Spirit is at work in believers now only in a preliminary way. The new age is still the age to come. The present age is an evil one. Christians must still live with their sin and mortality. Thus the Christian life is a life of penitence. But the Christian witnesses limits set to this sin and mortality, and the Spirit is the promise of complete deliverance with the total coming of the new age. And so Christian existence is a life of hope, as well as a life of penitence.

3. *Eschatology as a problem*

An exposition of these implications does not thereby, however, guarantee their general acceptance. This was made evident by our study of three contemporary interpretations of the New Testament. Especially in regard to the eschatological aspect of Paul's doctrine of the Spirit, the reactions ranged from total rejection by Dr Schweitzer, through antipathy to the futuristic elements in it and emphasis on what is already fulfilled by Professor Dodd, to a complete reinterpretation by Professor Bultmann. Considering the place Pauline doctrine holds in Biblical and systematic theology, such reactions to his eschatology are bound to have far-reaching consequences for Christian thought as a whole. Nor are these reactions simply the opinions of experts isolated by their specialisation from the stream of the everyday thought and life of their fellows. Quite the contrary, for it is common to these three men that they have had their fellow men in view as they worked, and precisely for their sakes they have felt it necessary to react as they have to Paul's eschatology. If they have judged the mind of their time correctly, we can only conclude that for contemporary thought eschatology is a problem which needs to be faced if the Biblical message is to remain credible.

In the first place, Biblical eschatology is often ignored because of the distraction from the proper responsibilities of life that it has been to some enthusiastic groups in the Church. One thinks, for example, of the popular movement of William Miller, who predicted the return of Christ on 23rd April 1843. In the case of such apocalyptic sects their reading of the Bible becomes dominated by the question when the end will come. As an attempt to find a definite answer to this question, contemporary happenings are interpreted as links in a chain of events which leads inevitably and quickly to a predictable consummation.

There is a strain in the New Testament which encourages this attempt at the composition of a cosmic time-table. Sample passages are: Matt. 10.23, 24.14 (and Mark 13.10), 24.34 (and Mark 13.30); Luke 21.28, 31. This reading of signs of the times and speculation about chronology is found in Paul—2 Thess. 2.3-8, 1 Cor. 7.26, 29, Rom. 13.11, 12. But the same New Testament contains in its witness a second strain which criticises the first and replaces it. These passages reserve to the Father the knowledge of when the end will come, and insist that the end will be a surprise to all—Matt. 24.36, 42, 44, 25.13; Luke 17.20, 21; and in Paul, 1 Thess. 5.2ff. If, then, we hold to this view of the matter, the first objection to eschatology is avoided by recognising the fact that God has in His sovereignty reserved to Himself the knowledge of the time of the end and that human curiosity is out of bounds at this point.

A second common objection to Biblical eschatology is that it has an enervating effect upon man, making him content with evil and injustice in the present by placing salvation in some future age, in which it will be brought in by the will and power of God alone. This is a much more serious objection to Biblical eschatology than the first we have mentioned—not because any basis for it can be found in the New Testament authors, but because this objection so seriously misses the theological point of eschatology. Eschatology as the consummation of salvation in the future by the power of God without the help of man expresses in terms of history precisely the same point which the Reformers sought to recover in the doctrine of justification by faith alone. This doctrine, too, was opposed on the grounds that it was destructive of good works and encouraged ethical laxity. But, properly understood, it has just the opposite effect by setting the believer free from the impossible burden of earning his own salvation and at the same time setting him free for loving obedience which was otherwise impossible. Thus, too, Biblical eschatology makes possible a striving against evil which does not hesitate at failure because the ultimate victory is God's and is assured. To modify or dispose of New Testament eschatology to meet this objection would be to compromise an essential truth about the nature of redemption.

This objection also misses the point that with the coming of the Spirit a transforming power is released which already conforms life to the model of the future consummation. Thus this objection probably springs either from a desire to effect redemption by human effort or from a too exclusively futuristic, one-sided understanding of eschatology.

One of the commonest objections against Biblical eschatology is that its keynotes are doom, destruction, and judgment. Here we have to do with a caricature of eschatology. Every function of the eschatological Spirit we have noted has been one of redemptive transformation. The life principle of the future age is positive and creative. Eschatology pronounces a 'no' only upon that which refuses to take part in this new creation and thereby loses its place in that future. Perhaps a recovery of the Pauline connexion between the Spirit and eschatology would remove the predominately sour taste which the mention of eschatology often arouses.

Finally, perhaps, the commonest of all objections to Biblical eschatology is that it is simply incompatible with modern thinking, a form of thought too strange to permit communication. And yet Communism, with its dominant eschatology of a future classless, ideal society, continues to win and hold converts among those who consider themselves to be the most modern and scientific of men. Perhaps what this objection really boils down to is that eschatology is merely unfamiliar to modern men— a strange, because empty, thought-form. If this be so, the Church is itself guilty of neglect. The preaching and teaching of a faithfully Biblical eschatology in its proper relations, and with the proper emphasis, could rediscover to the Church of our day a forgotten or misunderstood dimension of the gospel. To attempt to overlook eschatology is to leave it to the fringe groups and probable distortion. Better to put eschatology in its proper light, for the Bible will be read and its eschatology is unavoidable.

We have shown that with regard to Paul's doctrine of the Spirit, certainly eschatology is unavoidable. If we are inclined *a priori*, for the sake of our contemporaries, to dispense with it or reinterpret it for them, perhaps our contemporaries should be allowed first to examine for themselves the eschatology of the Bible in its raw form. Only then shall we really know whether or not they find it incomprehensible or unacceptable. Then we could discuss eschatology *with* the Church instead of *for* the Church.

BIBLIOGRAPHY

BARRETT, C. K., *The Holy Spirit and the Gospel Tradition*, Macmillan Co., New York and London 1947.

BARTH, KARL, *The Doctrine of the Word of God*, VOL. I, PT. I, T &. T. Clark, Edinburgh 1936.

BAUER, WALTER, *Griechisch-Deutsches Wörterbuch*, Alfred Toepelmann, Berlin 1952.

BEHM, JOHANNES, "*Ἀρραβών*', in Kittel, *q.v.*

BEYER, HERMANN WOLFGANG, 'Der Brief an die Galater', *Die Kleineren Briefe des Apostels Paulus, Das Neue Testament Deutsch*, VOL. VIII, Vandenhoeck & Ruprecht, Göttingen 1953.

BIEDER, WERNER, *Gebetswirklichkeit und Gebetsmoeglichkeit bei Paulus, Das Beten des Geistes und das Beten im Geiste, Probevorlesung am 19 November 1947, vor der Theologischen Fakultät der Universität Basel.*

BLASS, FRIEDRICH, and ALBERT DEBRUNNER, *Grammatik des neutestamentlichen Griechisch*, 9th edn., Vandenhoeck & Ruprecht Gottingen, 1954.

BORNKAMM, GUNTHER, '*Μυστήριον*', in Kittel, BAND IV

BROCK, WERNER, introduction to MARTIN HEIDEGGER, *Existence and Being*, Henry Regnery Co., Chicago 1949.

BUECHSEL, FRIEDRICH, *Der Geist Gottes im Neuen Testament*, C. Bertelsmann, Gütersloh 1926.

BULTMANN, RUDOLF, *Der Begriff der Offenbarung im Neuen Testament*, J. C. B. Mohr (Paul Siebeck), Tübingen 1929

——— 'Bultmann replies to his Critics,' in *Kerygma and Myth*, ed. Hans Werner Bartsch, S.P.C.K., London 1953, pp. 191-211.

——— '*Die Geschichtlichkeit des Daseins und der Glaube*', in *Zeitschrift für Theologie und Kirche*, J. C. B. Mohr (Paul Siebeck), Tübingen, 1930, 11. Jahrgang, Heft 5, pp. 339-64.

——— 'History and Eschatology in the New Testament', in *New Testament Studies*, Cambridge Univ. Press, London, I (1954), pp. 5-16.

——— 'New Testament and Mythology,' in *Kerygma and Myth*, p. I.

——— 'Das Problem der Hermeneutik,' in *Glauben und Verstehen*, J. C. B. Mohr (Paul Siebeck), Tübingen 1952, BAND II, pp. 211-35.

——— 'A Reply to the Theses of J. Schniewind' in *Kerygma and Myth*, pp. 102-23.

——— *Theology of the New Testament*, London, S.C.M. Press, 1952, VOL. I.

——— '*Ζάω*—Der Lebensbegriff des NT', in Kittel, BAND II.

BURI, F., 'Zur Diskussion des Problems der ausgebliebenen Parusie,' in *Theologische Zeitschrift*, Verlag Friedrich Reinhardt, Basel, 3 Jahrgang (1947), Heft 6, p. 426.

BURTON, ERNEST DE WITT, *The Epistle to the Galatians*, International Critical Commentary, T. & T. Clark, Edinburgh 1921.

CULLMANN, OSCAR, *Christ and Time*, S.C.M. Press Ltd., London 1951.

—— 'Das wahre durch die ausgebliebene Parusie gestellte neutestamentliche Problem', in *Theologische Zeitschrift*, 3 Jahrgang (1947), Heft 3, p. 178.

—— *The Earliest Christian Confessions*, Lutterworth Press, London 1949.

—— *Koenigsherrschaft Christi und Kirche im Neuen Testament*, Heft 10, Theologische Studien, Herausgegeben von Karl Barth, Evangelischer Verlag U. G. Zollikon, Zürich 1950.

DEISSNER, KURT, *Auferstehungshoffnung und Pneumagedanke bei Paulus*, A. Dichert'sche Verlagsbuchhandlung, Leipzig 1912.

DELLING, GERHARD, ''Ἀπαρχή', in Kittel, BAND I, pp. 483-4.

DIBELIUS, MARTIN, *An die Kolosser, Epheser, an Philemon*, J. C. B. Mohr (Paul Siebeck), Tübingen 1953.

—— *An Die Thessalonicher I II, an Die Philipper*, J. C. B. Mohr (Paul Siebeck), Tübingen 1952.

DILLISTONE, F. W. , *The Holy Spirit in the Life of Today*, Canterbury Press, London 1946.

DODD, C. H., *According to the Scriptures, the Substructure of New Testament Theology*, Nisbet and Co., London 1952. (A revision of a course of lectures delivered in March 1950.)

—— *The Apostolic Preaching and Its Developments, with an Appendix on Eschatology and History*. Hodder and Stoughton, London 1936. (A course of lectures delivered in 1935—appendix read on 24th October, 1935.)

—— *The Epistle of Paul to the Romans*, (The Moffatt New Testament Commentary), Hodder and Stoughton, London 1932.

—— *History and the Gospel*, Nisbet and Co., London 1938.

—— *New Testament Studies*, Manchester University Press, Manchester 1953. (The two papers under consideration are 'The Mind of Paul: I', 1933, and 'The Mind of Paul: II', 1934.)

—— *The Parables of the Kingdom*, Nisbet and Co., London 1935. (Based on a course of lectures delivered in spring 1935.)

FOERSTER, WERNER, 'Κύριος im NT', in Kittel, BAND III.

FUCHS, ERNST, *Christus und der Geist bei Paulus*, J. C. Hinrichs'sche Buchhandlung, Leipzig 1932.

GAUGLER, ERNST, *Der Roemerbrief, Prophezei*, Teil 1, Schweizerisches Bibelwerk für die Gemeinde Zwingli-Verlag, Zürich 1945.

GREEVEN, HEINRICH, *Gebet und Eschatologie im Neuen Testament*, (Neutestamentliche Forschungen, Dritte Reihe, 1 Heft), C. Bertlesmann, Gütersloh 1931.

GRUNDMANN, WALTER, 'Δύναμαι, Δύναμις—Der Kraftbegriff des NT', in Kittel, BAND II.

GUNKEL, HERMANN, *Die Wirkungen des heiligen Geistes*, Vandenhoeck & Ruprecht, Göttingen 1899.

HEADLAM, A. C., see WM. SANDAY.

HEIDEGGER, MARTIN, see BROCK, W.

HEINZELMANN, GERHARD, 'Der Brief an die Philipper', *Die Kleineren Briefe des Apostels Paulus*, (*Das Neue Testament Deutsch*, VOL. VIII), Vandenhoeck & Ruprecht, Göttingen 1953.

Héring, Jean, 'Saint Paul a-t-il enseigné deux résurrections?' in *Revue d'histoire et de philosophie religieuses*, (Faculté de Théologie protestante de l'Université de Strasbourg), 1932, pp. 300-20.

Holmstroem, Folke, *Das eschatologische Denken der Gegenwart*, C. Bertelsmann, Gütersloh 1936.

Kennedy, H. A. A., *The Theology of the Epistles*, Gerald Duckworth & Co. Ltd., London 1919.

Kittel, G., *Theologisches Wörterbuch zum NT*, W. Kohlhammer, Stuttgart 1935.

Koegel, Julius, "Ὁ κύριος τὸ Πνεῦμά ἐστιν', in *Aus Schrift und Geschichte* (theological essays presented to Adolf Schlatter on his 70th birthday), Calwer Vereinsbuchhandlung, Stuttgart 1922.

Kuemmel, Werner Georg, *Verheissung und Erfüllung*, Zwingli-Verlag, Zürich 1953.

Lietzmann, Hans, *An Die Galater*, (*Handbuch zum Neuen Testament*), 3rd ed., J. C. B. Mohr (Paul Siebeck), Tübingen 1932.

———— *Korinther I/II*, 4th edn., J. C. B. Mohr, (Paul Siebeck), Tübingen 1949.

———— *An die Römer*, 4th edn., J. C. B. Mohr, (Paul Siebeck), Tübingen, 1933.

Lohmeyer, Ernst, *Die Briefe an die Philipper, an die Kolosser und an Philemon*, 10th edn., Vandenhoeck & Ruprecht, Göttingen 1954.

Michaelis, W., *Reich Gottes und Geist Gottes nach dem Neuen Testament*, Friedrich Reinhard, Basel 1930.

Michel, Otto, *Der Brief an die Römer*, Vandenhoeck & Ruprecht, Göttingen 1954.

Nygren, Anders, *Commentary on Romans*, S.C.M. Press Ltd., London 1952.

Preisker, H., *Geist und Leben*, C. Bertelsmann, Gütersloh 1933.

Reinhard, Wilhelm, *Das Wirken des heiligen Geistes im Menschen nach dem Briefen des Apostels Paulus*, Herdersche Verlagshandlung, Freiburg im B. 1918, pp 20-1.

Sanday, Wm., and Headlam, A. C., *The Epistle to the Romans*, International Critical Commentary, T. & T. Clark, Edinburgh 1914.

Sasse, Hermann, 'Αἰών' in Kittel, band I, p. 197.

Schlatter, A., *Die Theologie des Neuen Testaments*, Vereinsbuchhandlung, Stuttgart 1909.

———— *Gottes Gerechtigkeit, Ein Kommentar zum Römerbrief*, Calwer Verlag, Stuttgart 1952.

Schlier, Heinrich, "Ἐλεύθερος—Der Begriff der Freiheit im NT', in Kittel, band II.

———— *Der Brief an die Galater*, (Meyer Series), 11th edn., Vandenhoeck & Ruprecht, Göttingen 1951.

Schweitzer, Albert, *The Mysticism of Paul the Apostle* (English translation of *Die Mystik des Apostels Paulus*), A. & C. Black, London 1953.

———— *Paul and His Interpreters* (English translation of *Geschichte der Paulinischen Forschung*), A. & C. Black, London 1912.

———— *The Quest of the Historical Jesus*, (English translation of *Von Reimarus zu Rede*), A. & C. Black, London 1911.

93

SCHWEIZER, EDUARD, *Geist und Gemeinde im Neuen Testament und Heute*, Chr. Kaiser Verlag, Munich 1952.

────── '*Πνεῦμα*', unpublished MS for Kittel, op. cit.

SOKOLOWSKI, EMIL, *Die Begriffe Geist und Leben bei Paulus*, Vandenhoeck and Ruprecht, Göttingen 1903.

STRACK-BILLERBECK, *Kommentar zum Neuen Testament aus Talmud und Midrasch*, C. H. Beck'sche Verlagsbuchhandlung, Munich 1926.

VOS, GEERHARDUS, 'The Eschatological Aspect of the Pauline Conception of the Spirit', in *Biblical and Theological Studies*, by members of the Faculty of Princeton Theological Seminary, Charles Scribner's Sons, New York 1912.

WEISS, JOHANNES, *Der Erste Korintherbrief*, 9th edn., Vandenhoeck & Ruprecht, Göttingen 1910.

WILDER, AMOS N., *Eschatology and Ethics in the Teaching of Jesus*, Harper, New York 1950.

WINDISCH, HANS, *Der Zweite Korintherbrief*, Vandenhoeck & Ruprecht, Göttingen 1924.

SCOTTISH JOURNAL OF THEOLOGY
OCCASIONAL PAPERS

General Editors: T. F. Torrance and J. K. S. Reid

———◆———